Thy Will Be Done . . . Eventually!

Alex Annand
&
Joan Histon

Illustrations: Philip Spence

Front cover photograph: David Mallams

ISBN 1 85852 140 8

© 1999 Trustees for Methodist Church Purposes

C3 1 80

'My legs ache, ma, they really ache.'

'You're not havin' another day off school, Alex, I mean it! It's growing pains, that's all, growing pains.'

My two younger sisters eyed me suspiciously from the kitchen table where they were finishing their porridge.

'I really do feel bad, ma,' I persisted.

Turning from the kitchen sink she gave me a stern look as if to determine how much was truth and how much a child's natural desire to escape school, then wiping her hands on her pinny she lifted the thick brown mop from my forehead to gauge my temperature.

'Mmm, you're very hot and you do look a bit peaky,' she admitted, her Scottish brogue softening. 'Perhaps we'd better take you to see the doctor. But mind you, Alex, if you're telling me fibs . . !'

'No, ma, I'm not, honest!'

'Mmm.' Still not totally convinced, but deciding she'd better not ignore the symptoms or my complaining, nor the fact that her usually noisy, boisterous son had been quiet and withdrawn all week, she set about hustling my sisters off to school. Then, tying a scarf around her head and pulling on an old navy coat which had outgrown its usefulness for warmth, she wrapped an extra scarf around my school mac and we braced ourselves against the cold, fine drizzle descending on the busy streets of Aberdeen.

Every step of the long walk was agony. My legs ached and constantly threatened to buckle under me, and the sweat poured off my forehead as I tried to keep pace with my mother.

'We'll soon be at the doctor's. Not far now,' Mam said, anxiously pulling me along behind her.

Although I hated being ill I enjoyed being in the doctor's waiting room where I could kneel on the chair and watch the ships wending their way up and down the river past the cranes and factories. But it was the shipyards where my dad worked that fascinated me. They had their own distinctive smells of oil, grease, metal and pungent river and I longed to be well again and for the war to be over so I could be allowed back through the great big gates to watch the ships being built. If it hadn't been for the tight security nothing would have kept me out. The shipyards were a family tradition. My grandfather, his sons and brothers had always worked in them and, since the war, my aunts had too.

'Mrs Annand? Doctor will see you now.'

Mam took my hand and trailed me through the overcrowded waiting room to an overworked doctor's surgery where the single bar of an electric fire did nothing to keep the chill from my aching, feverish body. Shivering, I stripped off and jumped as a cold stethoscope was planted on my chest.

'I don't know what's the matter with him, doctor. He's been in bed for a week and he's so peaky . . .'

'Mmm, take a deep breath, laddie,' the doctor said, moving the stethoscope to my back.

'He's so skinny, doctor, there's not a pickin' on him. Normally he's noisy and full o' life, but recently he's not had a lot o' energy. Growing pains, I've been telling him. You don't go to the doctor's for growing pains, but it does seem to be getting worse.' 'Another deep breath, laddie.' The stethoscope moved back to my chest.

'If he could just have a bottle, doctor. Something to keep him from complaining about the aching joints.'

'Bottle! Growing pains!' the doctor retorted angrily. 'Fishwives' tales! I'm afraid it's far more serious than that, Mrs Annand. Unless I'm much mistaken, the laddie's got rheumatic fever. He should have been to see me weeks ago!'

'Rheumatic fever! But . . . how . . ?'

The doctor walked over to his desk and as he began writing his tone softened. 'I don't know how serious it is, Mrs Annand, but as well as rheumatic fever I'm not too happy with the condition of his heart. I want you to take him to the hospital straight away and give them this letter. I'll ring for a taxi for you.'

'Taxi! We can't afford a . . .'

'For goodness sake, woman!' he snapped, throwing his pen on to the desk. 'Get it into your head. Your son is ill. Very ill!' He picked up the telephone to order the taxi and, still shaking, I struggled back into my vest, watching my mother's face turn white. I wasn't sure if it was from thoughts of the taxi fare to the hospital or the news that I had heart trouble and rheumatic fever. The seriousness of the doctor's tone scared me. How ill was I? Very ill? As in . . . dying? Dying to my eight year old mind conjured up visions of spiders with their legs torn off, bees buzzing frantically in an airtight jar or the rat poison our cat ate. Dying didn't belong to a young boy like me with his whole life ahead of him.

The doctor ushered me and my mam into the taxi and despite feeling so poorly a tiny thrill of excitement ran through me. This was indeed a rare treat. No-one ever got in a taxi in our street. You had to be rich to get a taxi – or dying!

'Ma?'

She patted my hand absently; the other, clutching her best hankie, trembled. 'We'll stop off home first, Alex, and get your dad. He'll know what to do. He'll have gone to bed after his night-shift, but that can't be helped.' She sat with tear-filled eyes staring out of the window at the familiar streets, unable to cope with the situation.

3

It was lunchtime and the kids in the street were home from school. They stared in amazement as we pulled up at our door and crowded round the taxi.

'Stay here, Alex. I'll get your dad.'

'Ma, don't . . .' She jumped out of the taxi and hurried to the front door leaving me alone and frightened on the big leather seat. I pressed my nose against the cold pane of glass. Tears rolled down my cheeks and my body ached intolerably.

A grubby fist appeared on the other side of the glass and began to grind the splodge that was my nose.

'Och, Alex! What are y' doing in a taxi? You robbed a bank or something?' My best friend Jimmy's bright freckled face grinned at me through the taxi window.

'Jimmy, I . . . I think I'm dying, Jimmy.'

The contours of his face changed shape as he tried to comprehend the news. 'Dying?' His eyes opened wider. 'You canna be dying, Alex.'

'Aye, I am, Jimmy. It's ma heart. The doctor telt me ma.'

'But . . . but . . . dying?' He frowned thoughtfully. 'Does that mean we canna go to the matinee on Saturday, Alex?'

'Aye, I think so. They're taking me to the hospital now.'

Jimmy's mouth gaped open. 'Hospital! Och, Alex! Me Auntie Pat went there and she never came out!'

I nodded miserably. Jimmy and I had come to our own horrific conclusions as to what they'd done to his Auntie Pat.

'Hey, Alex. If you die, what'll they do wi y'? Do y' think y'll go to heaven?'

'I don't want to go to heaven, Jimmy. I want to stay here.'

'But, Alex, if y' die and don't go to heaven, the only other place is . . .' The grubby fist swivelled around and an ink-stained thumb with a chewed nail pointed to the ground. I wiped the tears on my cheeks. What'd you mean?'

'You know That place!' He cupped his hands around his mouth and breathed 'HELL' through the window, leaving a mist on the pane where he promptly wrote his name.

Heaven or hell. Of course I knew about them, having gone to Sunday school, but God and the Devil rated in the same category as Auntie Bessie who lived in Glasgow, smelt of moth balls and lavender and went to church on Sundays. They were for old folks. For a wee boy such as me, heaven, hell and God were remote and unrealistic.

Our front door slammed and my dad, a wool scarf pulled tightly around his neck, his jacket and trousers on top of his pyjamas and his peaked cap slightly crooked, stepped into the taxi with a carrier bag. As we pulled away I saw Jimmy's face crinkle up and heard him sob, 'Alex! Alex! Y' canna die, Alex!' before the taxi turned the corner and we sped away.

My dad reached over and pulled me towards him. 'Dinna worry, lad. The doctors'll sort it all out.' The roughness of his jacket smelling of grease from the shipyards rubbed against my face, giving me a strange sense of comfort and I welcomed this unexpected show of affection from him.

'Am I going to die, dad?'

'Not if I can help it, laddie,' he said gruffly. After a pause he said, 'You know, Alex, when you were a wee bairn I found you in your cot one night turning blue. Aye, blue.' I'd heard the story before but I let him continue. 'I picked you up and shook you, trying to make you breathe, but you wouldna'. So picking up a bottle o' whisky I poured it down your throat. Aye, lad, what a mess! You threw up all over your mam's new mat, but it did the trick. You breathed again! If your guardian angel saw fit to save you once, he'll save you again, of that I'm sure.' The worried look on his face, however, did nothing to reassure me.

A nurse came to greet us as we drove up to the Sick Children's Hospital. I winced with pain as they lifted me on to a trolley, and as they wheeled me away down the long corridor I turned in time to see the stocky figure of my father standing in the reception area, brushing away the tears on his face with the sleeve of his jacket.

'Let me live, God. Please let me live!' was the frightened prayer I uttered through chattering teeth.

I lay for a long time staring at the familiar brown stain on the ceiling above my bed, memorising every mark and blemish for the last time. A tremor of apprehension surged through me as I thought about tomorrow. I turned over, curling up tightly to squash it, my gaze falling on Ben sleeping in the next bed. Ben was a year or so older than me, the veteran of the ward, bedridden with rheumatic fever and a severe heart condition. On the day I'd arrived in hospital, frightened, lonely and in pain he had taken me under his wing.

'Hey, Alex! If you stop your crying I'll give you one of my comics to read,' he'd said, and he'd opened the door of his locker to reveal rows of neatly-stacked comics in perfect condition.

I'd turned a tear-stained face towards him.

'These are special comics, very special comics. Not your Beano or Dandy,' he'd informed me with pride. 'These come from America and I don't let anybody read 'em, but if you stop your greetin' I'll lend you one.'

Curiosity got the better of me and, wiping a runny nose on my pyjama sleeve, I'd nodded. Ben wrapped an elastic band around a colourful comic and tossed it in my direction, and for a while I was lost in a fantasy world of monsters, aliens and super-heroes. But then the pain in my legs had started up again and turning my face into the pillow I'd cried myself to sleep.

When I awoke the following morning a nurse was stooping over my bed with the breakfast trolley. She was a large, buxom, rather forbidding figure. 'Come on, Alex, let's have a wee smile from you,' she said.

Fearful of what would happen if I didn't comply, I forced my mouth into a line and gave her a watery smile. I don't think it came up to her standards because she bent down

7

and whispered in my ear, 'If you give me an even bigger smile I'll give you an extra slice of warm toast.'

'That's Sister,' Ben explained later when she was out of earshot. 'She doesn't have a proper name. She's just Sister Jackson and she's a real dragon!'

I tried not to think of those first few weeks. They were a blur of doctors prodding and probing, needles and blood samples, pain, medication and an intolerable smell of antiseptic which seemed to infiltrate everything. I grew unnaturally quiet and withdrawn and a great sense of loneliness engulfed me when I found out that visiting was only permissible monthly, and then only from parents.

Although we were not church people, my mother had taken it into her head to send us children to Sunday school and somewhere among those Sunday afternoon visits, between tormenting the girls and getting into mischief, something must have sunk in, because I turned to God as the only available form of comfort.

'I don't want to die before I see mam and dad again,' I wept silently into the pillow after 'lights out'. 'Please God, don't let me die.' I racked my brains for some sort of bargain offer that he couldn't possibly refuse. 'I'll do anything! Anything! I won't ever hit our Eileen again and . . . and I'm sorry I broke our Kathleen's doll, but if you keep me alive and let me see my sisters again, I'll never, never be nasty to them again!'

Whether it was the medical treatment or an answer to prayer I'll never know, but over the next three months the pain and discomfort eased and as I began to feel more like my old self I conveniently forgot about God and the promises I'd made. The awful medication continued and I wondered how anything so vile could possibly be aiding my recovery. Ben reckoned that if they took any more blood out of me they'd soon have more bottles of it than I possessed in my body.

Eventually I was allowed out of bed for a short while each day and discovered that the hospital had wonderful places to explore.

'Go and see what's in that room at the end of the corridor,' Ben challenged me one morning. 'I've been watching them take jars of something through that door for months now but Sister won't tell me what's in there.'

'No. I'm nae gann in there, Ben. I'll never get past Sister Jackson.'

'Go on, Alex. Please!' Ben's big brown eyes turned pleadingly towards me. 'If you crawl under all the beds you'll get past her.'

'Well, I dinna think I could crawl, but I might be able to wriggle on ma stomach,' I said uncertainly.

Ben beamed. 'If she asks where you are I'll say you're in the toilet. And Alex, when you come back I'll give you one of me comics!'

This was a prize indeed. Ben's comics were his most treasured possession and held in high esteem in the ward. I needed no further enticement and two minutes later was crawling on my belly under the beds past the desk where Sister Jackson sat on sentry duty. I reached the open door at the end of the ward. In a second I was through and on my way to the room that held so much fascination for Ben.

The corridor was quiet at this time of the day. Reaching the door which hid unimaginable secrets I found a gap in the blind conveniently at my eye level. I peered through at long tables holding rows and rows of test-tubes and bottles and my eyes grew wide with excitement. There was more than just blood in some of those bottles. There was . . . there was . . . 'Wow!' I breathed in an awed voice. 'This must be where they put Jimmy's Auntie Pat!' Silently I turned the handle, heard the catch click and watched as the door slowly creaked open.

'Alex Annand!'

9

Every nerve in my body jangled. 'Aahh!'

Sister Jackson bore down on me like an overweight dragon in white. 'So you think you're well enough to be allowed to roam around the hospital do you?' she said sternly. I nodded dumbly.

'And you want to poke and pry around every room?'

I shook my head, clenching my teeth to stop them chattering.

'Mmm. Well, perhaps we can put you to some use. Tomorrow.' There was a twinkle in her eye and her voice softened. 'I think you've had enough excitement for one day.' She gently took my hand and led me back into the ward, but I knew at that moment that the dragon of our ward, Sister Jackson, had a heart and that I had found a special place in it which I unashamedly used at every available opportunity to twist her around my little finger.

Firmly tucked up in bed once again I delighted in describing the full gory details of the bottles of blood and guts to Ben and our imaginations did the rest to frighten us out of our wits! From then on our ward changed from being tolerable to pleasurable. I was a hero, the one who had 'escaped'. And in relating the room of horrors escapade to my fellow ward mates I discovered that they clamoured for more juicy tales, true or otherwise, and I was only too happy to oblige.

As I began to feel better I became more active and chirpy and for the first time in many weeks started singing:

> The bells of St Mary's,
> I hear they are calling,
> The young ones, the true ones,
> Who come from the sea . . .

'This is a hospital, Alex, not a concert hall,' Sister Jackson admonished sharply. Giving her a cheeky grin I made my way to the table in the centre of the ward, which was covered in books, crayons, comics and papers, and in a high pitched voice continued with verse two. I knew Sister Jackson liked to hear my boy soprano voice. She shook her head in mock desperation. 'If you're that keen on singing, Alex, how about helping us with the music for the Christmas festivities?'

I stopped in mid-verse and looked up, surprised. 'OK. Great!'

Christmas Eve was a memorable time and one which helped to ease the pain and loneliness of that first Christmas away from my family and friends. The ward was cheerfully decorated with a Christmas tree with bright lights, and presents strewn underneath. Nurses in their crisp white uniforms and red cloaks carried flickering candles as they walked past the beds singing carols. When they came to 'Silent Night', my solo voice rang out clear and sharp around the ward and everybody cried.

Tomorrow it was going to be hard leaving this place where I'd become a popular figure with the doctors, nurses and all the ward staff. Ben, other children on my ward and the regular hospital routine had brought stability to my life which had been turned upside down with sickness. But now the powers that be had decided I was well enough to be discharged and had arranged for me to spend a few weeks in a convalescent home on the outskirts of Aberdeen before I returned home.

'It's a lovely place, Alex, you'll like it,' Sister Jackson said as she packed my small suitcase. 'All that fresh clean country air is just what you need to regain your strength.' She folded my pyjamas neatly. 'Your mam and dad will be able to visit often. You'll like that, won't you, eh?' She turned her back as she placed them on the top of the pile but the tone in her voice had done nothing to reassure me.

Ben had been watching silently from the next bed. 'Do you think they'll send me there, Sister?' he asked hopefully.

She deftly pushed in a pair of socks and closed the lid before answering cautiously, 'That's up to the doctor, Ben,

11

but no doubt Alex'll come back to visit you. Won't you Alex?' I nodded, wishing I could pack Ben and Sister Jackson in the case and take them with me.

There were hugs, small gifts and forced cheerful farewells as I sadly left all that had become familiar over many months and embarked on the journey to the children's convalescent home in the special bus, with two or three other children. I pressed my nose to the window pane, absorbing the naked trees, grey skies hanging heavy with snow and fields brown and empty. More than a whole summer had passed since I'd entered the hospital, and I'd missed it all.

Deeper into the countryside we drove, the roads curving and dipping through the hills. Eventually the driver pointed ahead. 'There it is,' he said and, turning the bus into a narrow entrance, drove down the long winding track. He pulled up at a big old house, bleak and uninviting, with 'Moorfield' painted on a dilapidated board outside. The paintwork was dark brown, and drab curtains hung at the windows. I gave voice to the growing concern in my mind. 'Where's the nearest bus stop for my mam and dad?'

The driver chuckled. 'Och, it's not too far away, laddie. About a mile and a half down the road. Dinna worry, they'll be here to see you at the weekends, that is if it doesna snow. Terrible roads these are in the winter.'

I left the bus with my suitcase and the other newcomers and stood forlornly on the steps, the cold wind stinging my face and bare legs.

'Come on, in you come!' The lady who ushered us in was smart, efficient and obviously stood for no nonsense. I liked the look of her even less than I liked the look of the convalescent home with its plain glossy cream and green walls. She led us along a corridor reeking of polish to the office where she took further details, then up the stairs to the dormitory, past a small group of children who stared at us curiously. I stared back, disturbed by their thin bodies, institutional grey clothes and spotty faces. I didn't relish my recovery amongst these sick, pasty-faced children. If I'd looked in the mirror I'd have seen they were but a reflected image of myself. Little did I realise what a puny child I'd become lying in hospital all those months and how much I resembled them.

I was left in a sparsely furnished dormitory to unpack and meet my new room-mates, then led to the dining hall where I discovered the joys of greasy mince, bland unsalted mashed potatoes and tasteless vegetables. I soon became used to the constant smell of cabbage which haunted every room in the house.

My earlier fears of having no visitors were quickly realised when the snow arrived and cut us off from the outside world. At times the loneliness and sense of isolation was unbearable as week after week I sat at the window with the other children watching the flakes fall silently on to the fields and hills around us. The only sign of movement came from the local farmer or one of his sheep. Sometimes we would draw or read or I would take up my old flair for storytelling and relate with great relish imaginary tales of past occupants gruesomely murdered in this large cold, draughty establishment. They added to our entertainment and helped ease our loneliness, but they gave the younger children many sleepless nights and got me into trouble more than once.

A long, slow thaw set in and we waited anxiously for the roads to clear and the first signs that there was life outside the convalescent home. Mam and dad were among the first to arrive, wrapped up warmly to keep out the cold and armed with presents of clothes, comics and sweets. With a sob I flung myself into my mother's arms and buried my head into the nape of her neck, letting the tears fall unashamedly down my face on to the familiar navy coat and wool scarf.

'I hate this place!' I sobbed, 'I hate it!'

She wrapped her arms around me, holding me very close.

'There,' she soothed. 'There, there.'

I clung very tightly to her. It was such a long, long time since I'd been cuddled.

* * * *

Mam and dad, concerned about my unhappiness and the fact they hadn't been able to visit because of the distance and bad weather, decided I should go and stay with my grandparents who lived in the country. It would give them the opportunity to visit most weekends and give me the first taste of home life for many months.

'Hey, Alex! Are y' coming out to play?' I looked up from the breakfast table in my grandmother's warm kitchen as one of my cousins charged in through the door. 'Hi, granny.' Davey was a year or so older than me. 'Can Alex come out and play? It's nice and warm. Say yes, granny.'

I looked at her hopefully.

'His mam and dad sent him here to rest, Davey. Rest! Runnin' around with you's gonna tire him out.'

'Oh no, granny. I'll no' go far. Just a wee walk with Davey,' I urged. 'I'm getting stronger every day what with your good cooking and the fresh country air. Mam said I looked much better when she visited last weekend.'

Granny chuckled. 'You've got a silver tongue in your head, Alex. Aye, you might as well go and give my ears a bit o' peace from your infernal whistling. I rue the day your grandpa taught you how! Go on wi' y', and mind, don't tire yourself.'

I let out a whoop of joy, hurried to the cupboard under the stairs to get my coat and then ran out of the door with Davey. Within minutes we had joined his friends and were racing to the old disused quarry and the special corner they had cultivated for themselves with scraps of metal, old tyres, rocks and numerous coded signs which, when

14

interpreted, threatened torture or death or worse to trespassers. To this den and its robbers I was sworn in and spent the morning happily skimming stones across the deep water from the top of the quarry.

'Hey, Alex, let's see if we can move this cart.'

I looked up to see Davey standing on an old discarded cart. I grinned, my mind immediately inventing exciting adventures for our new-found toy.

'OK. It looks a bit wobbly, though.'

'It's quite safe. Been here for ages. Climb up.'

'Aaahh . . . It's shaking!'

'Dinna fret, mon. You're doing fine.'

'We can make this our special camp, Davey.'

'Aye, if you can get yersel' up here we can! Come on. That's it!'

It was only a slight movement. No-one expected my foot to slip between the wheel and brake, and that it should do so just as the cart moved was most unfortunate. There was an excruciating pain in my left heel before I blacked out.

'. . . but Mr Annand!'

'No! I'm no' havin' Alex go there, and that's final!'

My ears pricked up at the mention of my name, my interest aroused by the unusually dogmatic tone in my father's voice. Pushing back the bedclothes I slid out of bed and quietly crawled across the bedroom floor. I opened the door slightly and peered through the slit towards the raised voices in the room opposite where the school welfare officer was engaged in conversation with my parents.

'Mr Annand, your son has missed months and months of schooling, first the time he spent in hospital, and now there's the problem with his foot.'

'Aye, but he's much improved recently.'

'Perhaps, but since the accident to his foot he's had to be carried everywhere. We can make arrangements for him to attend a special school for children with . . .'

'No! He's going to no special school!' I'd never heard my father speak to anyone in authority quite so firmly before.

The welfare officer could hardly contain his frustration. 'No one in their right mind would expect a boy with osteomyelitis in his foot, a history of rheumatic fever and heart trouble to attend an ordinary school and be expected to participate in games! A special school for delicate children like Alex would take such things into consideration!'

'Delicate! My son's not delicate and he's been pampered long enough! As soon as the doctors have fitted a block to his plaster he'll be walking, then afore you know it his plaster'll be off and he'll be fit for normal school! Gettin' all the right treatment is our Alex.'

The welfare officer sighed. 'All right, Mr Annand. Have it your own way. But I don't know how you expect him to cope with the rigours of school life. I have to say that from my understanding of the situation your son may be left with a permanent limp. Have you taken that into consideration?' There was an ominous pause before the welfare officer continued. 'You have to accept the fact that his illness, then his accident have resulted in a great loss of schooling. Obviously he's a long way behind other children.'

'Perhaps we should listen to what they have to say,' interrupted my mother nervously.

'Maggie! Quiet! He's not going to a special school and that's final!' There was a short pause, then I heard my father's chair creak as he stood up. 'Our son isn't any different to anyone else. I'll have him back to school soon and he's a bright enough lad to catch up. Now I thank y' for your concern but he's my son and I know what's best for him.'

I gripped the side of the door, curbing the overwhelming desire to cheer. It wasn't so much my dad's apparent victory over the welfare officer that delighted me, it was more the fact that he had displayed, in this heated conversation, a greater love and concern for me than I'd ever known before.

The following morning my breakfast tray was late. I sat up in bed waiting for it to arrive, listening to Kathleen and Eileen arguing about school books and my mother urging them to hurry or they'd be late. Finally I heard Eileen racing across the hall with the crockery rattling on the tray.

'You're late!' I admonished. 'And have you put sugar in my tea?'

'Oh no,' she groaned.

'Well, I need sugar in my tea, stupid!'

17

'Then get it your lazy self!' she snapped. 'You're turning into a right spoilt brat, our Alex! No wonder you've no friends left!'

I stuck out my tongue as she marched out of the bedroom slamming the door behind her, but her words had a ring of truth about them, which hurt. I was loving the constant attention from my mother. I had to be carried everywhere by my dad and uncles because I wasn't allowed to walk. I received sweets and comics from doting relatives, with which I took great delight in taunting Eileen and Kathleen. Sickness, I discovered, was fine, but, in spite of all the attention, I had to admit it had its drawbacks. Jimmy and other friends called but I could see that they soon became bored with the restricted indoor games I was capable of playing and their eyes would stray longingly to the window where they could see the other kids kicking a football around in the street. Their visits had grown less frequent as the weeks dragged on and I was beginning to feel isolated and lonely. I could see my parents were concerned that I no longer whistled and chattered incessantly but had become irritable and frustrated.

The day the block was fitted to the foot of my plaster was the turning point. It gave me a new sense of freedom. I could walk; I even ran once I got used to it and when no one was looking. I spent so much time on my feet I soon wore the block down, but regular visits to the hospital to have it replaced gave me the opportunity of visiting Ben.

'Hi, Sister.'

Sister Jackson looked up from her desk where she was busy writing. 'Hello, Alex. I didn't expect to see you today. You're not back already for a new block to your plaster are you?'

I grinned. 'I wore the other one out.'

'I'm not surprised with all the running around you do. Where's your mam?'

18

'In the waiting room. She said I could come to the ward to visit Ben.'

'Alex, I . . .'

'Where is he?'

I looked across the ward towards Ben's bed but it was empty and freshly made up. His locker, usually piled high with comics, books and drinks, was cleared. I sensed a hesitation in Sister Jackson and fleetingly recalled how poorly Ben had been on my last visit.

'No! No!' I turned to Sister Jackson for the slightest glimmer of hope that I was wrong but her eyes were swimming with tears. 'I'm sorry, Alex. I'm so sorry. Ben died yesterday.'

A lump the size of a football grew inside my chest, threatening to explode. Sister Jackson placed a consoling hand on my shoulder and I gave vent to my heartache, allowing the tears to flow unhindered.

I grieved deeply for Ben in the weeks that followed but it seemed as though everybody had lost somebody at the end of the 1939-1945 war and my loss was no greater or no less than anyone else's. My mind returned frequently to those special comics that had been like gold on our ward, to Ben's kindness in sharing them with me on the day I'd arrived, his sense of fun and the strong bond of friendship that had grown up between us. I couldn't help but wonder why God had let such a good person like Ben die while someone like me, who couldn't even keep a few simple promises, like not fighting with his sisters, had lived.

It was after six o'clock one evening. I'd idled the day away making paper pellets to flick at our Eileen when she returned from school, only to discover she'd saved some of her sweets for me, so the pellets had been surreptitiously stored for another occasion. There was a clatter of boots in the hall marking my dad's return from work. He looked tired as he came in through the door, almost as tired as my mam had looked recently.

'You all on your own, lad? Where's your ma?'

I shrugged my shoulders. 'Kitchen, making dinner, I think.'

He eased himself into the chair by the fire and began to unfasten his boots. 'Your mam says you're walking better each day, our Alex. Is that right?'

I nodded. 'It's painful sometimes, though.' It wasn't really, but I was reluctant to give up all the attention I was getting.

'Aye, lad. It's been a long sickness.' He leant back in his chair surveying me thoughtfully. After a pause he said, 'We'll have you back to school, I think.' I didn't say anything.

'You canna beat a good education, Alex. I dinna want you doing the same job as me and your uncles. There's no future in labouring. You want a good white collar indoor job and for that you need to get back to school.'

'But I canna run and play games like the other lads, dad.'

His big hands reached out to the warmth of the fire and there was silence before he answered. 'You will, lad. If you really want to. Perhaps you need to try a bit harder.' I lowered my eyelids, comparing my small hands with his.

'You've gotta learn to be strong, Alex. Fight back. Don't give in to your illness.' Give in? I wasn't giving in to my illness, was I? I'd been sick, injured, nearly died! We sat in a thoughtful silence, my dad and I, then he said, 'Do you understand what I'm saying to you, son?'

I nodded dumbly.

'You gotta learn to stand up and be a man, Alex. You canna spend all your life lettin' the women folk wait on you.' He rubbed his hands together. 'Right!' That's all I've got to say on the subject. Now then, Maggie! Where's ma dinner?' Standing up, he followed the smell of his dinner into the kitchen.

A few weeks later I was back at school, although I tired easily and as I still had a plaster on my leg I wasn't expected to take part in any of the sports. I took great delight in taunting my friends as they set off on their cross-country runs on a wet day.

During the summer holidays I had my plaster taken off and returned to school in September to find a new sports teacher in the gym.

'Annand! Why aren't you in your PE kit and boxing gloves?' he barked. The eyes of the whole class turned in my direction.

'Sir, I . . .' I swallowed hard, hating the attention drawn to my inability to join in games. 'Sir, I've been ill. I'm excused games.'

'Sir, Mr McKie, sir,' said the form prefect, 'he's a cripple. They usually let him sit and watch.'

Ex-Sergeant McKie, recently demobbed from the army, eyed me suspiciously. 'Can you walk, Annand?'

'Yes, sir.'

'Can you run?'

'Yes, sir. A bit, sir.'

'Do you want to get fit and well?'

'Yes, sir.'

'OK. Well, let's get one thing straight. I don't have shirkers in my class. Got it? Go and change into your PE kit and get a set of boxing gloves!'

Angry and embarrassed I turned and limped across the gym, feeling the eyes of the class on my receding figure. I was actually quite good at exaggerating the limp which I could put on at will to gain a sympathetic audience. Once in the changing room I slammed the door in a spate of fury. How dare he show me up like that! He hadn't nearly died! How would he like to spend months and months in pain

21

having doctors prod and poke you, stick needles into you and take your blood? How would he like to be shoved away from his home and family, and then be called a cripple?

As I exchanged a warm woolly school uniform for a light cotton PE kit I inwardly seethed. 'I hate him!' I muttered, but somewhere inside I knew that wasn't true. There was something about this new PE teacher that I liked and I desperately wanted him to like me.

Slowly and thoughtfully I made my way back to the ring of boys in the gym where Jimmy tied the boxing gloves for me. They weighed heavily on my thin arms. My skinny white legs shook with cold under the long black shorts which flapped around my knees and the white T-shirt hung shapelessly around my painfully thin body. 'Do you want to get fit and well?' he'd said. Stupid man! Of course I wanted to get fit and well so I could race around like the other kids. But sickness and pain seemed to have been part of my life for such a long time now I couldn't imagine what it must be like to be a normal, active boy and not get out of breath after running a few yards. 'Be strong and fight back,' my dad had said. 'You gotta fight back, Alex!' Had I really turned into a weakling, accepting sickness as a normal part of my life? 'A spoilt brat!' Eileen had called me. 'No wonder you've no friends left!' It hurt to think that she could be right, but if she was, how could I go about changing things?

'Right, boys! Who'll come into the centre and be my sparring partner?' Mr McKie's loud voice echoed alarmingly around the gym. No one moved. 'Volunteers!' The new PE teacher bounced up and down in the middle of the circle of boys, his gloves raised for action. 'Who'll take me on?'

The class backed off, slightly apprehensive of the menacingly athletic ex-sergeant, fresh from active service in the war. However, one small boy, his skinny white legs protruding beneath extra large black shorts and a marked lack of muscle on his body, raised his boxing gloves in the air in a gesture of defiance. 'I will, sir! I'll take you on!'

The long fight back had begun.

℀ 4 ℁

Under the tuition of Mr McKie, my boxing skills developed. Unfortunately the practices weren't always restricted to school hours or premises.

'Come on, Alex! Dob 'im!' Jimmy turned me round and shoved me back into the centre of the ring of boys gathered in the corner of the church graveyard. Blindly I swung my right fist, my knuckles skimming off my opponent's Brylcreemed hair as he ducked. He retaliated with a left hook to my right eye. Half-blinded, I stumbled back against his jeering companions. The blurred image of his red sweater advanced.

'You're gonna get it, Annand!' he growled. 'I'll teach you t' nick my lass!'

My breath came in short, sharp rasps. An unexpected blow sent a spurt of blood from my nose over his sweater. Dazed, I staggered back against one of the gravestones. Ever the optimist, I was about to finish him off when a frantic whisper circled around the group of spectators.

'The minister! Let's get out of here!' Jimmy grabbed my jacket collar and dragged me along behind him over the gravestones and out of the church premises into the street.

'Alex! Jimmy! You boys! Are you fighting after Sunday school again? Come here at once! Do you hear me? At once!'

'He must be joking,' Jimmy panted. 'He'd skin us alive if we went back!'

Once out of sight we slowed to a gentle jog then took a short cut through the back lanes, where Jimmy examined my injuries.

'Och, Alex. You're a right mess.' He pulled a dirty, ink-stained hankie from his pocket and proceeded to wipe the blood from my nose. 'She wasna worth it.'

'I know that!' I retorted. 'But I'm sick o' that Harry McLaren getting at me. Ouch!' Jimmy dipped the hankie in a puddle and pressed it to the swelling below my eye. 'He's picked on me all through school!' I stormed. 'Now he's after my girlfriend.'

'What y' talking about? She wasna your girlfriend.'

'That's besides the point,' I snapped, pulling strings of chewing-gum off my eyelashes. 'He needed teaching a lesson.'

Jimmy snorted. 'I don't quite know who taught who what lesson, Alex, but it's you that's the bloody mess and been threatened with expulsion from the Sunday school if you keep causing trouble.' He savagely dabbed the end of my nose. 'You're gonna cop it when your dad sees that eye.'

Fortunately dad was out at the pub when I sneaked in through the kitchen door and mam was asleep in the chair by the fire. Kathleen and Eileen stared in horror at my grotesque appearance but, out of fear of my threatening fist, kept silent.

I arrived at school the following day quite proud of my rugged appearance. 'That's a real shiner you've got there, Alex,' Jimmy said admiringly as we made our way up to the second floor. It was Open Day and we were acting as monitors, directing parents to the various classrooms on our floor. 'What did your dad say when he saw it?'

'I didn't see him, so I didn't tell him. If I had he wouldna understand me fighting over a girl at Sunday school. He'd have given me another lickin'. I sneaked out of the house early this morning and when I see him tonight I can say . . . well, I'll think of something.'

'It'd better be good.'

'Aye, I know. I dinna want to miss Sunday school. Did you see that new lass on Sunday?'

'Och, aye.' We leant on the rail at the top of the stairs, drooling over the latest addition to the Sunday evening teenage group at church. Church had an awful lot to offer these days.

'Do you think I should invite her to the Sunday night mission?' I ventured.

Jimmy looked at me despairingly. 'Och, Alex! You do have some daft ideas at times. Y'canna ask a girl for a night out serving pie and peas to the drop-outs of Aberdeen. Take her to the pictures or something.'

'Aye, perhaps if I've enough cash I will, otherwise she'll have to wait till I'm earning. Just think, Jimmy, in a few weeks we'll be out working.'

We stood in silence for a while, engrossed in our own thoughts. These last years at school hadn't been so bad, I reflected. Under the intense tuition of the ageing Mr Catto and Mr Ironside, I soon had a firm grasp of most subjects, and with Mr McKie's encouragement in sport I now had more confidence in my physical abilities. Now in this, my final year, I felt proud of my achievements. Not only had I become head boy but my final year exam results had surprised even me. 'You boys got nothing better to do than lounge over that rail looking untidy?' Mr McKie barked as he marched towards us.

'Not really, sir,' I answered, averting the most gruesome side of my face.

'Mmm. I want to see your parents when they arrive. OK? That's quite a shiner you've got yourself, Annand. Not fighting, I hope?'

'Who, me, sir? No, sir!'

He continued walking briskly down the stairs towards the first arrival of parents who were looking lost and bewildered at the rows of corridors they would have to negotiate before finding their child.

'You sure your dad's not coming to the Open Day?' Jimmy asked when Mr McKie was out of sight. 'I dinna want to be around when you cop it.'

'Dead sure. He's never been to a school Open Day in his life, so he's not likely to start now.'

'Dead sure, huh? Look!'

'What?' I leant over the banister. Below stood a stocky man with a familiar cloth cap. 'I canna believe it! It canna be!' But I knew I could never mistake that cloth cap. I looked at Jimmy in horror. 'Me dad!'

'I telt y', Alex. You'll cop it for that black eye.'

Apprehensively I watched the cloth cap ascend the stairs towards us.

'What'll I say?'

'We could . . . you could say er . . . er . . .'

'Yes? Yes?'

'I dunno, I canna think in such a short space of time.'

My father's face remained expressionless as he reached the top of the stairs and took in my black eye.

'Hi, dad. What you doing here? Where's mam?'

My father straightened his tie. 'Seeing as how this is your last Open Day before you leave school, I decided to come, Alex. I want a word with the teachers about your future. Now. Where do I begin?'

Jimmy eyed us both warily, then backed into the corner. In an uncomfortable silence I led my dad along the corridor to my classroom which was empty except for Mr Catto, Mr Ironside and Mr McKie. All three stared at my black eye.

'Dad, er . . . this is Mr McKie, who takes us for games, Mr Catto, the English teacher, and Mr Ironside.'

Mr Ironside and dad eyed each other silently for a moment.

'You'll not remember me,' dad said, 'but I remember you well.'

'Oh?'

'Aye. You taught me.'

'Did I really?' Mr Ironside peered intently at dad.

'Aye, you did that, sir.' The two men shook hands like long-lost pals.

'Well, now, isn't that the thing!' How've you been doing over the war, lad?'

Lad? Lad? It was hard to imagine dad being a lad. Thankfully the black eye was forgotten as the four men launched forth with their reminiscences of the war: Dad and the bombing in the shipyards, and Mr McKie with this famous 'cooking eggs on the tank in the blistering heat of the desert' yarn which we pupils used as a ploy to sidetrack him from the business of teaching. I stood silently in the background wondering when they would come to the focus of their meeting – me!

'The lads still have a nickname for me,' Mr Ironside concluded, 'Don't they, Annand?'

I surfaced from my wandering thoughts. 'Er, yes, sir.'

'And it's what, Annand?'

' "Tinners", sir.'

My father chuckled. 'Aye, in my day it was "Tin-ribs". By the way,' he suddenly remembered the reason for his visit, 'How's our Alex doing?'

All eyes swivelled to gaze intently at me and my gruesome face.

'He's caught up fast,' said Mr Ironside. 'Worked hard, very hard.'

'Aye,' agreed Mr Catto. 'He's not a brilliant scholar, never will be, and I doubt he'll make university standard, but considering all the setbacks he's had, he's no' done so bad. Reached the top class, made head boy and he's reliable, very reliable.' He frowned at my black eye. 'Usually,' he added. 'Usually.'

'He's no longer poor Alex with the limp,' chipped in Mr McKie. 'Staff and boys alike are all impressed with the way he's overcome his physical difficulties.'

'Aye, he's a real credit to you,' said Mr Ironside warmly.

'Hrrump!' Dad noisily cleared his throat and said gruffly, 'Aye, aye, well, that's fine to hear, Tin-rib . . . er, Mr Ironside, sir. Fine to hear. Thank you for your time, gentlemen, and all the help you've given our Alex here.'

I gave Jimmy the thumbs-up as dad and I left the classroom.

'He's OK is old Tin-ribs,' said dad as we made our way down the stairs to the entrance hall. 'Take heed of what he tells you, Alex mind.'

'Yes, dad.'

'And the least said about the black eye the better.'

'I got it . . .'

'I know where you got it, lad, and Sunday school isna the place to fight – ever – especially over a lassie!'

My mouth dropped open in surprise. 'How did you know . . ?'

He struggled to suppress a smile. 'Never mind how I know.' He glanced at his watch. 'Well, I'll be off now then.' He turned abruptly and made his way across the playground without a word of goodbye. Thoughtfully I stood on the school steps watching him. There'd been no 'Well done, that was a good report.' No sense of pleasure at my reliability, not even a tirade of anger over my black eye, and it was a mystery how he'd found out about it. He was a hard man to understand, was my dad. There were hidden depths I had yet to fathom out. With confused thoughts I made my way back to the classroom for the last two weeks at school.

* * * *

Jimmy and I had a night out at the pictures to celebrate.

'I canna see.'

'There! Over there!'

'It's too dark, Jimmy. I canna see a bloo . . .'

'Would you two lads sit down so the rest of us can see the film! This is a cinema not a football match!'

'Oh hell!'

The usherette's torch flashed angrily in our direction. 'You boys! Shut up and find a seat!'

Jimmy herded me along a crowded row of seats, ignoring the occasional yelp of pain as we ground someone's toe into the floor.

'We'll get seats right behind them, Alex,' he hissed. 'I'll have the blonde one, you can have the other.'

I peered through the gloom of the picture hall. 'Where are they? I canna see what mine looks like!'

'There! In front!'

'I wish I'd got some popcorn,' I muttered as we took two seats in the middle of the row behind two girls with heavily lacquered beehive hairdos.

'We're not here for popcorn, Alex. We're here to try and get off with the two lassies in front, and mind, don't forget, mine's the blonde one.'

I wasn't quite sure what Jimmy had in mind. Girls in the form of a physical attraction had crept into my thoughts frequently in my last school year but I had neither the courage nor the know-how to do very much about it.

'I think I'll get some popcorn, Jimmy.'

'Stuff your popcorn, Alex. The girls . . !'

'I'll not be long.' Rising to my feet I shuffled along the row of exasperated cinema-goers and a few minutes later, armed with an enormous packet of popcorn, trampled them underfoot again as I shuffled back to my seat.

'Ouch!'

'Get off ma . . .'

'Sorry.'

I sat down and tore open the packet of popcorn.

'Shhh . . .'

I slumped down, digging my shoes into the back of the seat in front where the blonde sat. She glanced behind warily, gave me the once-over, then inclined her head towards the brunette to whisper, blocking my view of the screen. Then both heads turned and their stares developed into stifled giggles.

Jimmy gave me a nudge. 'Smart move, Alex.'

I wasn't sure what I'd done but I gave Jimmy the thumbs-up, dived into my popcorn and turned my attention to the mutant on screen which had wrapped its tentacles around the slender body of a shimmering sylphlike beauty. I munched my popcorn in fascination, my eyes growing wide with excitement as she struggled to escape its fleshy, gaping mouth. Suddenly a dashing hero in skin-tight leathers darted out of the undergrowth, his ray gun aimed at the mutant's solitary eye. I held my breath as the mutant's tentacles moved provocatively over the squirming female body. Yet I wasn't totally absorbed; my attention was momentarily drawn from the screen to a shaking leg pressed firmly against mine. I wriggled uneasily in my seat then gave Jimmy a sly nudge in the ribs.

'There's something not quite right with the fella next to me. His knee won't stop shaking against mine.'

Jimmy tore his eyes away from the screen and looked across me to the man at my side. 'Do you think he has shell-shock?' I whispered.

31

Jimmy leant back, grinning broadly. 'He's not got shell-shock, Alex,' he whispered. 'You're sitting next to a poof!'

The shaking stopped and a hand rested on my knee. I held my breath. Meanwhile the sylphlike beauty on screen fainted and the beehive hairdos in front gasped with excitement.

Nervously I turned to Jimmy. 'Jimmy. What's a poof?'

He told me. My fingers froze over the bag of popcorn. Warily I turned to stare at the man sitting next to me. He smiled as one confidant to another, gave me a slow wink and moved his hand just as the hero in tight trousers fired into the mutant's solitary eye. It roared with pain. I roared with fear and disgust and leapt out of my seat. The popcorn bag exploded and sticky popcorn rained down over the heavily lacquered beehives in front.

'Oh, Alex! How could you?' Jimmy squirmed in his seat as the girls leapt up with yells of alarm. Grabbing my jacket, Jimmy and I made a quick exit along our complaining row of cinema-goers and dived up the aisle into the gents' toilets, leaving two angry girls picking sticky popcorn out of their hair.

We walked home from the cinema in brooding silence until we came in sight of the old bridge down by the canal. I grabbed Jimmy's arm.

'What?'

'Look!'

The popcorn splattered females were not more than a dozen yards in front.

'You dinna think they'll take any notice of us after your fiasco tonight, do you?' Jimmy admonished.

'I thought you said the blonde one was always willing?'

'Aye, well, we'll soon find out.' He ran a comb through his hair. Jimmy had his patter all rehearsed. I think he'd learned it from his older brother and it must have worked, for a few minutes later they were walking alongside us. At least part of it worked. I had the blonde, Jimmy had the other one.

I racked my brains for a suitable topic of conversation. 'Did you enjoy the picture?' I ventured, pleasantly aware of her jacket brushing against my arm as we walked.

'Picture? Oh, yes. Till some dunderheed hurled popcorn all o'er me and Sandra!'

'Oh!' The blood rushed to my face but the darkness hid my embarrassment. I racked my brains for another topic of conversation but all that came to mind was what came into view. The inane rambling about the old tyres at the bottom of the canal must have impressed her for as we made to go under the old bridge she took my hand. Her fingers were cold and sticky, from the popcorn I assumed, as she drew me into the shadows of the bridge. Jimmy and his lass walked on, their heels echoing around the arches. Darkness engulfed them, leaving the blonde and me silent and alone. I could feel her hot breath coming close to my neck. I put my arm awkwardly around her shoulders and . . . and . . .

'Hey, Alex! Alex!'

I deliberately didn't hear.

'Alex! Hey, Alex!'

Reluctantly I unwrapped myself from the sticky, fleshy mouth, untangled my fingers from the heavily lacquered hair and popcorn and growled, 'What d'you want?'

'I wondered if you and er . . . what's 'er name fancied fish and chips?'

'Oooh! Fish and chips! Your treat, eh?' My blonde bombshell pushed me away, tutted saucily, readjusted what was left of the beehive, then tottered off giggling to join her friend. I followed her out of the darkness of the bridge giving Jimmy a sly nudge as I passed.

He grinned. 'Alex, did . . ?' I walked on. He could guess whatever he wanted but I felt good. Not because I'd managed to get his blonde, but because I was moving away from my protected boyhood into the real world of men – and it was great!

'How about it?' I said confidently, straightening my jacket. 'Fish and chips, eh, girls?'

During the years that followed the war there was a general recession all round and a lull in shipbuilding in Aberdeen. My father was forced to work short time, week on week off, which brought financial hardship to us and many other families. Even with my small wage coming in from Burton the Tailors there was barely enough to meet our needs. My uncle, who had left Aberdeen in search of employment, sent back glowing reports of the work in the shipyards of Tyneside and persuasive letters suggesting that my father should join him. And so it was that I was forced to leave an active social life in my beloved Aberdeen for the strange land and tongue of the Geordies, for so the folk on the Tyne were named.

Jimmy came to bid us farewell as the removal men packed our belongings into their van.

'I'll come and visit you, Alex.'

'Aye.' We stood in an awkward silence, unsure how to say goodbye without looking foolish.

'Or you could come and stay wi' me,' he volunteered.

'Aye, I could.' Another long silence.

'At least Burton's have transferred you to their shop down there, Alex. It could be worse.'

'Aye, I suppose, but as soon as I've enough saved I'll be back, for good. I'll not be stopping in England for long.'

'Aye.' Jimmy didn't sound too convinced. 'Meanwhile I'll write and let you know who they get to take your place as assistant leader in the junior youth club, eh?'

'OK.' I paused. 'Jimmy, I'll miss . . . the kids at the youth club and I'll miss . . . the lasses at church. We've had some great times there, eh?' We laughed awkwardly, shuffling from one foot to the other.

'Well,' Jimmy said, 'Your mam's waving for you to get into the taxi, Alex. Remember the last time you were in a taxi? You were going to the hospital and we thought you were gonna . . . aye well, you didn't, did you? Anyway, I'd better go. Write, eh?'

'Aye, I'll write.'

Jauntily turning on his heel he sauntered off down the street, giving a mock salute when he reached the corner. The last I saw of Jimmy was a mop of red hair disappearing around the brick wall.

The weeks following our arrival on Tyneside were unhappy ones for me. I'd known times of loneliness in hospital when I'd been removed from the security of my family and forced to face sickness and pain without their love and comfort, and again during the bleak winter in the strict institutionalised children's convalescent home. But here, crammed in a three-bedroomed council house with my uncle, aunt and their children, my mam, dad and sisters, I discovered a new kind of loneliness: that of having no space to spread my wings, no room for friends to visit, even if I had had any. There was no visible outlet for a teenager to let off steam or burn off energy and I became frustrated, withdrawn and quiet.

In late autumn dad found a job as steward in the local working men's club and we rented a house, but Christmas was a dreary affair with packing cases all around us instead of a Christmas tree and no grandparents or friends popping in.

After Christmas, however, there was at least some improvement. 'Would you like to come to the club with me tonight, Alex?' Dad was pulling his boots on when he asked the question.

I looked up, surprised. 'Pardon?'

There were a few grunts as he bent over to fasten his laces. 'Do you want to come and give me a hand behind the bar in

36

the club, lad? We're a bit short-handed. It's better than moping around here.'

I felt a surge of delight that my father actually wanted my company. 'Yes, dad. I'd like to come.'

So Sunday school, the mission and youth club were replaced by the working men's club with snooker, dominoes and helping my father serve behind the bar. I threw myself wholeheartedly into raising money for charity by starting a swear box, to which I was one of the biggest contributors. It gave me a warm glow to hear dad say, 'Ready, lad?' every Sunday evening when he woke from his half-hour nap after dinner and whatever the weather we'd don our shoes and set off together for the club. Sometimes we'd talk, but at other times there would be a companionable silence that would be interrupted by dad's mates when we arrived. That was the only problem, really. They were dad's mates, not mine. Even at Burton's, all the staff were married with families to go home to, so even though I took great delight in the developing friendship with my father, that first winter on Tyneside was a pretty lonely one.

I sat at the back of the bus on the way to work one morning, reading a letter from Jimmy. He was never very good at putting pen to paper and over the months his letters had become fewer and shorter. But this current one brought back happy memories of the youth club and the old life in Aberdeen. My thoughts were wandering into vague unrealistic plans of how I could return and pick up where I'd left off, when my dream world was rudely shattered by the monotonous crooning tones I'd been forced to listen to every morning on the bus for the past few weeks. A bad imitation of an Ella Fitzgerald song echoed around the upper deck accompanied by rapping fingers on the back of my seat. Irritated, I swivelled around. The noise stopped and a broad grin spread across the crooner's face.

'Hi! I see you on this bus every morning,' he said. 'You get off at the same stop as me. Where do you work?'

'Burton's, in Gateshead,' I answered. The prickles of annoyance rapidly disappeared; he had such a friendly, cheery manner.

'Why, man, you're just down the road from me. Shove over!' A lean, six-foot form shoved me along the seat so he could sit next to me. 'I'm George, by the way. George Brown.'

'Alex Annand.'

'Oh, aye? A haggis basher, eh?' he chuckled.

'A Scot, aye.' I grinned back.

'I work in an office at the Quayside, but not for much longer. The army, Alex. That's what I fancy. The army.'

'The army?'

'Yup. Great stuff, the army.' The next twenty minutes were lost in a debate over the merits and demerits of the various armed forces, a conversation that was revamped every morning on the bus on our way to work.

'How can you like the RAF better than the army, Alex? I tell you the army's the place. I'm gonna apply.'

'When?'

He shrugged. 'Soon. I've to sign up for National Service next month. How about you?'

I hesitated. I didn't relish the idea of having all my old ailments dragged up, then being turned down as unfit for National Service but I banished those negative thoughts from my mind when I said, 'Well, we all have to sign up for National Service sometime – it's the RAF for me, though.'

'Howay, Alex man, join the army wi' me. We'll see the world together.'

'Perhaps.' The idea certainly held great appeal.

A few weeks later I received my National Service papers. I didn't say anything to George because I wanted to get the first hurdle of the medical over and done with.

The doctor's examination room was cold and clinical, unpleasantly reminiscent of many others I'd been forced to sit in when I was younger. A large, bald-headed doctor flicked through my notes from behind his desk.

'You've quite a medical record here I see, Mr Annand,' he said. 'A weak heart, rheumatic fever, osteomyelitis. Dear God! And you expect to get into the army?' He looked at me as though I needed a brain transplant.

'Er . . . yes . . . yes, I do.'

'Mmm, well I suppose we'd better give you a thorough overhaul. Strip off!'

Overhaul was the right word. One by one my clothes were shed and every part of me was examined, tapped and listened to. Left in my birthday suit I was instructed to jog up and down while he critically assessed every moving piece of flesh.

'Mmm. Right! You can get dressed now.'

With a sinking heart I pulled on my vest, waiting to hear the obvious prescription of rest, medication and the name of a consultant.

'All clear, Mr Annand.'

I stood with one leg in my underpants wondering if I'd heard correctly. 'Pardon?'

He looked up from the papers on his desk. 'I said OK. You're fit. A1, passed for training.'

I pushed the other leg in the same hole. 'I'm OK? I'm fit?' I couldn't keep the surprise out of my voice.

A slow smile flickered across his face. 'That's what I said, lad. Other than a tendency to repeat my diagnosis like a parrot and being unable to dress yourself, that is.' He glanced over to where I stood with both legs through the same hole of my underpants. 'You're fit enough for the army to have you, lad.'

I stared at him, trying to take in words I had never heard in the whole of my life. I was fit! I was like everybody else, which meant I could do anything. Anything!

'A1 fit?' I repeated again. The words echoed sweetly in my ears.

'And I've a long queue of men yet to see, Mr Annand, so get a move on.'

'Oh! Right! Sorry.' Scrambling into my trousers and sweater I walked out of the doctor's surgery in a euphoric daze. There was a spring in my step as I made my way back to see the sergeant in the Army Recruitment Office to complete the papers that signed me up for army service for the next two years. George had finally convinced me that the army was the place.

I could hardly contain my exciting news when I met up with George later that evening. I waited until we'd settled ourselves in the corner of the pub with our pints before I produced my papers. 'I went for my medical today, George.'

'Oh, aye? Went to sign up myself today as well.'

'Did you? Great! The doc says I'm OK, fit, so I took your advice and I've signed up for the army.'

George's glass stopped mid-flight from the table to his mouth. 'The army? You've signed up for the army?'

'I have. I thought you'd be surprised. Look out, world, here we come!' I raised my glass towards him in a mock salute.

'But I thought you favoured the RAF?'

'I did, but then I got to thinking over what you'd said about joining up together and seeing the world.'

George put his glass down with a thud. 'Oh, Alex man. It's all official now, is it?'

'Aye. I'm only waiting for the papers of confirmation.' I frowned at his miserable face. 'What's up? Didn't you pass your medical?'

'Oh, I passed the medical all right. No problems there.'

'They'll put us in the same barracks, bound to,' I said, puzzled by his lack of enthusiasm.

'No, Alex, they won't. Not in a million years.'

'Why? What's wrong?'

'Well, I thought it would be great to see the world with a mate as well, so I signed up for . . .'

'Terrific!'

'. . . the RAF!'

I stared at him in disbelief. 'But, George, you'd set your sights on the army.'

He nodded. 'And you for the RAF.'

And so it was that out of friendship we went our separate ways.

◌ 6 ◌

'Welcome to Fenham Barracks, lads.' The sergeant smiled broadly at the small group congregated in front of the big double gates with their suitcases. 'Glad to have you with us.'

We smiled back, pleased to have the sacrifice we'd made in joining the army appreciated. 'Line up, line up,' he said, indicating where we should form two lines. We did as requested. 'And now,' his voice dropped an octave so we had to strain to hear his next words, 'I want to remind you where you are.' The warm smile vanished and the eyes narrowed. 'You're in the army now!' His tone in made my stomach sink into my boots. 'And what's the first thing you're going to do in the army?' The voice rose threateningly.

'Go home on leave?' muttered the slim young chap slouching next to me with his hands in his pockets.

The sergeant turned sharply towards us. 'I'll pretend I didn't hear that!' he barked. 'And I'll repeat, what's the first thing you're going to do?'

My companion remained silent and the two lines shuffled uneasily.

'You're going to get your bloody hair cut!' he bellowed. 'You're in the army, not the Girl Guides, and I'll not be having a shower of Nancys in MY platoon!' He began to inspect the front row. 'You! You! Get your hands out of your pockets! Stop slouching! Smarten up! Shoulders back! I'll make soldiers of you miserable lot if it's the last thing I do!' His contemptuous glare made us feel like naughty children having been discovered doing something we shouldn't. 'Pick up your cases. Attention! Right turn!' There was a moment of confusion while we worked out our left from our right but eventually we all faced the same way. 'When I say "quick march" I want you all marching to that far building and let's start by at least having you look like soldiers!'

Any glamorous pictures I may have had of the army rapidly faded as we marched from one hut to another, collecting our army kit and uniforms and having our hair cut. Eventually we were herded into the barracks which were to become our home for the next six months. I dumped my gear on the nearest empty bed I could find.

'What on earth have we let ourselves in for?' I said to no one in particular.

'God only knows.' The slim young joker who'd been standing next to me earlier threw himself on the bed next to mine. 'I'm Ronnie, by the way. Ronnie Palmer.'

'Alex Annand.'

A giant of a lad with muscles that made Tarzan look like a wimp took the bed on the other side of me. 'I'm Mick. Mick Johnson,' he said.

I very soon discovered both my companions had religious leanings. Ronnie vehemently expressed the name of Jesus Christ every time something wasn't to his liking, which was usually most of the time, while Big Mick never mentioned him at all, but every night, just before lights out, he would kneel down at the side of his bed and pray. At first there were a few snide remarks but because of his size no one dared openly mock his nightly ritual and I certainly had no intention of commenting on it. In fact I had a quiet admiration for his courage at being able to demonstrate his faith in such a way. I could never have done it in a barrack room full of blokes from so many different walks of life, many of them real rough diamonds.

I remembered the words of my dad and former old soldiers in the club where dad worked: 'Take your time in choosing your friends and watch your kit.' Sound advice. Things had a habit of disappearing and having to replace them was a strain on the meagre pay-packet.

I soon adapted to being part of a body of men. Swearing was very much a natural part of everyday life but that wasn't new to me having been brought up in the streets around the shipyards of Aberdeen. In the army, though, according to our instructors, we were all the illegitimate sons of somebody.

It was one thing being told I was A1 fit but proving it was something quite different. Standing next to Big Mick in my shorts and T-shirt waiting for instructions for the cross-country run, I was conscious of my skinny legs and scrawny body. I didn't think the sergeant was over-impressed either, by the dismissive way he passed me by. However, over the next ten weeks of training I discovered muscles my skinny body didn't know existed and the ability, not only to keep up with the others, but actually to pass red-faced, overweight soldiers gasping for breath. After a childhood of sickness no one can imagine my sense of achievement as I jogged back through the gates of Fenham Barracks with the first group of runners. I had not only proved I could do the training and keep up with the best of them, but that I was even better than some of them. I soon became very cocksure.

Towards the end of our drill, weapon and physical training, I arranged to go home for an evening and work at the club to give dad some time off. He and mam wanted to have a night out. Unfortunately I didn't reckon on our sergeant deciding on a cross-country run from Kenton Bank Foot, a rural area a few miles out of the city. It was a mere doddle for the local lads who knew all the short cuts back to the barracks, but for a lad from Aberdeen, still unsure of the area, it was a nightmare, especially when I was dumped in the middle of a field late in the foggy afternoon with Ronnie and Mick.

A cold blanket of silence engulfed us as the lorry lurched away through the mud to drop the next group of runners.

'Right, lads!' I gently jogged up and down in an attempt to keep warm. 'The first move is to get back to the road. Right?'

'Right.'

'You'll know the way from there, eh, Ron?'

Ronnie's vacant expression was the first indication that we were in trouble. 'What makes you think I'll know the way back?'

'You're a Geordie, aren't you?'

'Aye, but Newcastle covers a canny big area, Alex man, and I'm a Walker lad. That's on the other side of the city, a hell of a distance from Kenton Bank Foot!'

I turned to Mick who immediately raised his hands. 'Don't look at me. I'm from Northumberland.'

I stared at my mates, horrified. 'I thought if I had you two lads from the north I'd be sure to get home on time.'

'Standing where we are isn't going to get any of us back,' Mick said. 'I suggest we follow the tracks of the lorry. It's muddy enough. Then presumably we'll meet up with some of the city lads who'll help us get back to barracks.'

'Good idea.'

We set off over the ruts caused by the lorry. Mud and cowpats splattered up our legs and shorts as we ran. There was a great deal of cursing from Ronnie behind me. Suddenly a dark shape loomed out of the gloom, taking us all by surprise. Fortunately it had four legs and was chewing the cud.

'Hold it! Hold it!' Mick brought us to a grinding halt and the Ayrshire lifted her head, her curiosity aroused.

'What's up?'

'I've a feeling we've picked up tractor tracks and lost the lorry.'

Placing my hands on my hips I steadied my breathing and strained my eyes through the thick mist that had hovered around all day and now shrouded the landscape. 'If we could find a wall, that would help.'

'How?'

'Walls have gates. Gates lead on to roads,' I said confidently.

A few fields and gates later we reached a small country track with expensive houses either side. A solitary figure emerged from the mist with his dog. Relieved, we ran up, fending off an angry looking mongrel as we asked directions.

'Why, man, yer miles frum Fenham Barracks!'

We could have told him that! The bad-tempered mongrel snarled at my shorts.

'Yer wanna gan doon there . . !' He gave rapid instructions in his native dialect leaving me more bamboozled than ever, and Ronnie and Mick still confused even though they'd understood every single word. However, we thanked him, gave the mongrel a wide berth and set off in the last direction his finger had pointed, which was towards a housing estate.

The mist had now turned into a fine cold drizzle and the early evening dusk was making visibility difficult. On top of which the first pangs of hunger were pulling at my insides, reminding me that time was getting on and I didn't want to miss mam's steak and kidney pudding before going down to the club to stand in for dad.

'We're never gonna make it,' I panted.

'Yes, we will.' Ronnie stopped suddenly, causing a human pile-up. 'Didn't that fella say there's a short cut around here somewhere?'

'Did he?' Mick gazed around. 'All I can see is a maze of houses and fog.'

We surveyed our surroundings. Cars were pulling into driveways indicating the return of people from work. Lights shone in living-room and kitchen windows and delicious smells wafted through the air as families sat down to their evening meal.

'See those lights over there?' We followed Mick's pointing finger. 'I bet that'll be the crossroads.'

'And if it is how are we supposed to get there?'

'Simple! Aim straight for it.'

'What? Through all these back gardens?'

'I dunno about that,' I said apprehensively.

'I thought you needed to get home urgently?'

'Aye. I do.'

Mick slapped me on the back. 'No problem then. Just follow me, lads.' Without further hesitation he leapt over the nearest garden wall. 'Ouch! Oohh! Damn!' Ronnie peered over the wall, grinning. 'We're coming, but we'll take a detour round the rose-bed, Mick.' We followed him cautiously over the garden wall.

There was a bellow from the house. 'You lads! Get out of my garden!' In my haste to escape, instead of going back the way I'd come, I jumped over the hedge separating his land from his neighbour's. There was a loud splintering of glass as I landed with both feet through a low greenhouse window-frame. More lights came on and there were shouts of 'This is private property! Get **** off my land!' I heard Ronnie and Mick crunching glass underfoot. The next minute they'd hauled me out of the greenhouse and we were leaping over the wall into the next garden. Over fences, walls, bushes and empty flower-beds we raced, only stopping once more to haul Ronnie out of a goldfish pond. Panting and dishevelled we left the estate with echoes of 'We'll get the police after you lot!' throbbing in our ears.

There was a steady flow of traffic as we neared the main road. The rush hour was well underway. Anxiously I glanced at my watch. I was not only missing my dinner but was already late for giving dad a hand in the club.

'Look!' Excitedly I pointed to the first familiar sign in the last four hours. The welcome, bright yellow number 12 bus! The conductor looked up in surprise as three dishevelled, mud-splattered soldiers, cut and bleeding from glass and rose bushes and with a pungent smell of cowpats clinging to their shorts and T-shirts, leapt on to his bus.

'Fenham Barracks,' I panted, then realised with a sinking heart that we hadn't a penny between us.

The conductor held his nose and grinned. 'Divind worry, lads. I'll let ya hitch a lift, as long as ya stay on the platform in case the inspector gets on.' I think the idea of wreaking havoc on his overcrowded bus appealed to him.

Half an hour later, weary, wet, smelly, freezing cold and covered in 'clarts', we jogged through the barrack gates in tune to the sergeant's complimentary comments, 'Better late than never!' or words to that effect.

The dinner was burnt and dad was more than a little annoyed I'd let him down. I tried explaining what had happened but he brushed me aside as if I were a schoolboy. 'I expected you an hour ago, Alex,' he said, frowning.

'Aye. I'm sorry I'm late but there was this cross-country . . .'

'Your mam went to a lot o' bother cooking your favourite dinner and you promised me you'd help out at the club to give us a night off.'

'I couldn't help it. I got lost somewhere between Kenton Bank Foot and the barracks.'

'We're all dressed and ready to go out.'

'Sit down, lad. Sit down and get your dinner.' Mam bustled into the room from the kitchen with a hot plate of steak and kidney which was burnt around the edges. Hungrily I tucked in.

'Well, there's no point in going out now,' dad grumbled.

'Never mind. Perhaps you can come and help out at the club next week.' Mam's conciliatory attitude didn't make me feel any better.

'If you do, just make sure you're on time,' Dad said sarcastically.

'I can't make any promises,' I said between mouthfuls. I could feel my hackles rising with annoyance at his attitude.

'Oh, and why not?'

'Bugger me!' I snapped. 'I'm not a kid, I'm a **** soldier! I can't go taking time off to help you at the club! I'm sorry I'm late, but there's nowt you or I can do about it so . . . so if y' divind **** like it, dad, you'll have to bloody well lump it!' Too late I realised that swearing to that extent was something my father had never heard from me and, although he swore himself, it was something he would never allow in the house. I bent my head over the dinner plate hoping no one had noticed. There was an uncomfortable silence.

'Aye. Well. I'd better get away to work,' dad said eventually. 'I'm late already.' Mam remained quiet.

I helped dad in the club bar later on that evening before catching the bus back to barracks. It turned out to be a good night despite our earlier disagreement and there was soon quite a crowd around the bar listening to me embellish tales of army training. Out of the corner of my eye I saw my father quietly listening while he worked, occasionally taking a drink from his glass and laughing at my stories with the others. Although he would never say so I could see from the look on his face that he was proud of me and I glowed under his approval.

It was much later that night, as we walked from the club to the bus stop, before he mentioned the swearing. 'You know I divna mind you swearing, son,' he said. I glanced at him, surprised. I could remember many a wallop for my foul mouth when I was much younger. 'You've heard me swear afore, eh, Alex?'

I nodded.

'But never in front of your mam or sisters, lad. Us men folk use language not suited to their ears. Best kept that way.' He nodded his head as if to emphasise the wisdom of his own words. 'And I'd be obliged if you'd remember that, Alex.'

'Aye, dad. I will.'

I jumped on the bus with three words echoing in my ears. 'Us men folk!'

ℭℛ 7 ℰℴ

'Where's me mug?'

Mick looked up from the lower bunk where he was reading. 'Dunno.'

'Where the hell's it got to? I was drinking from it while we were playing cards. Then I went up on deck and now I canna find it!'

Ronnie and Mick attempted a half-hearted search, clearing up items of their belongings I'd strewn all around our patch but there was no sign of the small tin mug individual to our regiment.

'It's gotta be somewhere,' I insisted.

'Aye, but it's a bloody big troop ship to start pulling to pieces all for the want of a tin mug,' Ronnie grumbled.

A few minutes later I spotted it, half-hidden on the bunk of the Scouse I'd been playing cards with earlier that day. He and his regiment bunked alongside us on the crowded lower mess deck as we headed for Singapore. I hesitated. He was an unsavoury character and I had no desire to have a confrontation with him. The decision was taken out of my hands.

'Hey! You! What you doing by my bunk?' His tone was aggressive right from the start.

'This,' I reached over and pulled the mug from his kit, 'belongs to me!'

'Like hell it does! Keep your thieving paws out of my stuff!'

He was a big lad with a thick Liverpudlian accent and he glared angrily at me. 'Put it back, Jock!' He took a threatening step towards me.

51

'I don't want trouble,' I said, backing off and lifting my hands. 'Just my mug.'

He swore aggressively at me but I stood my ground, determined to keep things under control. Slowly he pulled a large switchblade out of his shorts' pocket and flashed it threateningly towards me, grinning broadly as he saw the apprehension on my face. This wasn't what I'd bargained for. All I wanted was my mug!

The knife sliced through the air, frighteningly close to my face. I could feel the panic rising as I reached out to grab it but suddenly sixteen stone of muscle threw me back against the side of his bunk. My head smashed against something solid and my temper flared. Now more angry than afraid, I hurled myself at him but he was agile for his size and retaliated with a heavy blow to my ribcage. I doubled up in pain, dropping the mug on the floor. He kicked it towards his kit and advanced towards me. Clenching my teeth I hurled my whole body towards him again and clung to the wrist holding the knife. We struggled. He was heavier than me, but I was wiry and anger added weight to my attack.

'Leave him be! Leave him be!' Mick's voice penetrated my fury and I found myself being dragged away from my attacker.

'Leggo! Leggo!' I fumed. 'Let me get at that Scouse bugger!' But Mick held on to me, giving the Scouse's mates time to relieve him of the knife and pin him to the wall. The rest of my platoon, hearing a scuffle, arrived to back me up and the two groups glared angrily at each other, neither anxious to start a regimental feud.

'Come on, Alex. It's not worth it,' Ronnie urged, pulling at my arm, but such was the anger that burned inside me that I was not to be deterred.

'That **** took my mug!' I stormed angrily. Both parties eyed each other uncertainly.

'Ours is the only regiment that's got mugs like this.' Eric, another of my mates, bent down to retrieve the object in question. 'Where did you get it?'

The Scouse shrugged, averting his eyes. 'Found it.'

'It's mine!' I snarled through clenched teeth.

There was an uncomfortable silence then the Scouse's body noticeably relaxed. 'Go on, you stupid Jock, you might as well have it. It's no **** use to me!' he said.

I couldn't believe he was giving in so easily. He brought his face close to mine and I recoiled at the foul breath. 'But don't think this is the end of it,' he hissed. 'And don't take too many walks on deck!'

It was only later I discovered he had noticed one of his officers approaching and was anxious to have the confrontation end, as he'd been in trouble for fighting before.

Eric thrust the mug at me then he and Mick dragged me on deck and left me to cool off. I found a reasonably quiet corner and put my head in my hands. After a while my anger began to subside and I stopped shaking. A warm breeze blew through my hair and I made a conscious effort to relax, listening to the sound of the engines, the laughter of the soldiers around me and the splash of the sea against the boat as it cut its way through the ocean. Me and my temper! It would get me into trouble one of these days. I couldn't help but wonder how Mick, a Christian, would have reacted in similar circumstances. He never seemed to get uncontrollably angry. For the rest of the journey, my mates took great care that the Scouse and I were never left alone together, and I was grateful for their support.

The days passed, and we finally reached our destination. Singapore! I leant over the rail of the ship savouring the atmosphere of sailing into this busy Eastern port. Scores of cargo ships and tankers of all nationalities and sizes lay in neat rows across the deep blue waters of the anchorage. Chinese 'kongkangs' or sailing barges, Malay sampans and pilot boats dodged our approach and brown, bronzed and yellow faces waved or called a friendly greeting to the soldiers who lined the decks.

I strained my eyes towards the approaching harbour. The tall white spire of a cathedral glistened in the morning sun. Ultra-smart hotels peered through small clumps of leafy trees and the harbour and river were lined with buildings. There were no domed mosques, pagodas or other elements of an eastern culture which I'd expected. As our company disembarked I was struck by the extraordinary colourful mixture of races. Chinese, Malay, Indians and the odd European milled around the harbour. It all seemed so remote from the war up country where we were headed to join our regiment in the big fight against Communism.

'God Almighty!' Ronnie Palmer wiped his brow with his sleeve. 'It's hot!'

I nodded, dropping my kitbag beside his. Mick stood grimly beside us, his body taut, the sweat running down his face. I sensed, rather than saw, that all was not well with him. 'What's up, Mick?'

For a moment he looked decidedly uncomfortable. Then he said stiffly, 'I'd rather you used different words to express the heat, Ron, OK?'

'What? What the hell are you talking about?'

It was the first time I'd ever seen Mick look even slightly angry. ' "God Almighty" means something different to me than it does to you,' he said gruffly. 'And I'd appreciate it if you kept that expression away from me.'

'But I've always bloody . . .'

'I know you have,' Mick interrupted. 'And I've put up with it, till now. All I'm saying is, curb it around me. OK?'

Ronnie shrugged.

'Look!' I interrupted the strained atmosphere and pointed to the three-ton trucks pulling up beside us. 'Transport's here.'

Ronnie was obviously glad to have the subject changed. 'Howay, lads, I'm dying for me dinner,' he said, grabbing his kit.

'Move it! Move it! Move it!' The sergeant's melodious tones echoed around the waterfront, making the onlookers jump and bringing an automatic response from those of us in uniform. Our time at Fenham Barracks had trained us to react to the slightest command and had transformed us from individual gangling lads into a smart body of men, trained to be a fighting machine, but nothing could have prepared us for the sweltering tropical climate of the Far East.

Squashed like sardines in the truck, our convoy made its way through the busy streets of Singapore. Old buses without any glass in the windows thundered through clean wide streets lined with palm trees. Curiously we noticed the British flag flying over a number of buildings. However, our driver was obviously not in the mood for sightseeing and drove rapidly towards our barracks.

'Look! Raffles!' Eric indicated the famous Raffles Hotel, not looking quite so elegant since the second world war.

'Changi!' Ronnie pointed a nicotine-stained finger in the direction of a huge bleak building which, during the war, had been a Japanese POW camp. In recent years it had been restored to its former use – a prison – and continued to look grim and uninviting.

We drove into the green and fertile grounds of our barracks, Selerang Garrison. Once this too had been an infamous Japanese POW camp but it had now been restored to a magnificent three-storey, white building, pleasantly laid out around three corners of a parade ground.

'Not bad, not bad,' Ronnie grinned at me. 'I don't mind acclimatising myself for the jungle here.'

During the following weeks we took every opportunity available to explore Singapore Island. We sampled the Singapore Sling 'Tiger beer' in one of the many colourful bars or nightclubs, and took advantage of the wide variety of Chinese, Malay or Indian dishes on offer on the food stalls, which meant we were eating anything from hot dogs, curry, bird's nest soup, satay or our favourite, which was chunks of chicken, beef or lamb barbecued and served with peanut butter and chilli sauce. We spent many pleasant hours wandering around Chinatown, filled with quaint stores and traditional Chinese homes with brightly painted wooden shutters over the windows. Parts of Chinatown were off limits but that didn't deter some of the servicemen from breaking the rules. I thought frequently of George Brown with his burning ambition to see the world. Poor George had been posted near Leicester with the RAF so I tried hard not to glamorise my lifestyle in Singapore when I wrote to him.

Most of the time, however, it wasn't glamorous at all. Those few weeks at Selerang Garrison were used to train us for jungle warfare and at the same time acclimatise us to the tropical heat, and woe betide anyone who was found suffering from sunstroke or sunburn. It was a chargeable offence to damage the Queen's property!

Ronnie managed to pick up a few Chinese and Malay swear-words to enlarge his own personal dictionary of foul language. Mick would just give him a slow wide smile and get on with the job in hand. That was what I liked about the guy: his easy-going manner. Nothing seemed to ruffle him. Other than the occasional 'damn' or grumble he enjoyed his work, avoided trouble and was a good soldier and mate.

It was building the new command post that upset him. This particular day we'd been digging holes in the ground, filling sandbags and arranging camouflage. The monsoons had come early, bringing a sudden downpour of warm rain and drenching everything in sight. Then our transport broke down and we had to walk back to Selerang Garrison in the torrential rain. Wet and exhausted we arrived at camp not in the best of moods.

'And I've got a blister,' Ronnie grumbled, sitting on the edge of his bed and gingerly removing his boot. 'Oh hell! Look at it!' He examined the bloodied mess around his heel.

'I've some elastoplast in my locker,' Mick volunteered. He had already discarded his wet clothes and was lying flaked out on his bed in his shorts contemplating the fan on the ceiling.

I put down my book. 'Don't let the sergeant see that foot,' I warned.

He pulled his other boot off. 'I don't believe it. There's another one on this foot! Jesus bl **** ****.' Hardly had the words left his lips than Mick leapt from his bed, his face contorted with rage. In a few short strides he rounded my bed and grasped Ronnie by the collar of his wet shirt, lifting him from his bed and pinning him to the wall. His feet dangled two feet from the ground. I leapt up, trying to stop what looked like the start of a very nasty incident, but it was like wrestling with a gorilla. The colour had drained from Ronnie's face.

'I'm not gonna tell you again!' Mick bellowed at the top of his voice. 'I'm not gonna have the name of MY Lord taken in vain like that! Do you hear me, Ron? Do you?'

'Yeah! Yeah! I hear you! You're choking me, Mick! You're choking me!'

Mick dropped him like a rag doll and he slid down the wall, landing in a crumpled heap on the floor. There was a stunned silence. What manner of man was this Jesus Christ, who could invoke such loyalty and passion in a gentle, easygoing man like Mick? It certainly put paid to my theory that church was for women, children and milksops.

Mick flung himself back on his bed and lay staring at the fan on the ceiling again. Ronnie remained on the floor, stunned. The awkward silence persisted. I decided I'd better be the one to break it. 'How about a trip to Chinatown for the evening?' I said with forced cheerfulness.

I thought at first they were both going to ignore me but then Mick rolled over and said, 'Good idea, Alex. I think a night on the town before we head up-country would do us all good. What do you reckon, Ron?'

Ronnie looked up. 'Oh, er . . . aye. Aye, good idea.' He nodded sheepishly.

Mick grinned. 'OK. First drinks on me, lads!'

ℂ℞ 8 ℘

' . . . then they took this poor old Malay guy, skinned him . . . then . . . roasted him alive! They said you could hear his screams . . . Damn! Not another stop!'

Our gruesome storyteller was silenced as the convoy of armoured trucks slowed to a crawl yet again. It wasn't a moment too soon for me. I had been forced to listen to his explicit horror stories of Communist atrocities against the occupants of Malaysian villages sympathetic to the British, for the last three hours, and was left in no doubt of the type of aggression we would be up against from these bandits.

Our convoy had left Selerang Garrison and Singapore early that morning and crossed the causeway into Malaya. We were replacements for our regiment engaged in fighting Communist terrorists hiding in the dense jungles of southern Malaya. The scenery had changed considerably once we'd crossed the causeway. Roads had become more like dust tracks. Cars and rickshaws were replaced by carts and bicycles and half-naked coolies stumbled under heavy loads towards large rubber plantations. The armed vehicles escorting us were a sharp reminder that we were moving into dangerous territory.

By midday the temperature had climbed to thirty-five degrees. Thick giant trees sheltered us from the sun but the humidity of the jungle brought a frenzied attack of mosquitoes and an uncomfortable prickly heat as the sweat rolled down our backs. Regular as clockwork came the roll of thunder followed by a heavy downpour. It cooled the air slightly but made the roads muddy for travelling. Eventually our lorry, straining in second gear, came to a grinding halt behind the rest of the convoy.

'Welcome to Kluang camp, lads,' the driver said with a wry smile.

One by one we rolled off the trucks and silently surveyed our new home. Heavy barbed wire surrounded what used to be a Japanese POW camp. It struggled to hold back the heavy dark-green jungle which threatened to engulf this tiny piece of civilisation. Lines of wooden huts, each housing about twenty men, filled the terraces of Kluang. These were to be our new quarters, while those on the lower parade ground, surrounded by white painted stones, formed the administration offices.

We found our way to the hut assigned to us and spent the rest of the day settling in. Later that evening I stood on the small veranda overlooking the compound which was still brown and muddy from the heavy rain. There was a continuous twitter of birds, crickets and frogs hidden in the damp heat of the jungle. This claustrophobic settlement brought only too vividly to mind the many men who had suffered here ten to fifteen years ago as prisoners of the Japanese. My heart sank at the thought of billeting in this God-forsaken place for the next fourteen months. Miserably I noticed that not even the British flag, hanging limp in the still, clammy air, could muster enough energy to give us a wave of welcome.

Never in my wildest dreams would I ever have believed that this place could feel like home, but after three days of tramping through the jungle on patrol, I would have given anything to be back at Kluang camp drinking an ice-cold beer outside our hut. I echoed my thoughts aloud to Eric who was tramping behind me.

'I thought you didn't like the hut?' was all he said.

Ronnie, in front of me, swung his machete vigorously at the heavy undergrowth.

'Anything's better than . . . this . . . place!' His aggression only served to add to the perspiration already soaked into his jungle-green kit.

'A nice dip in the river'll soon cool you off, lads,' the sergeant informed us from the front of the column.

I thought I'd heard the roar of heavy water in the distance. Now, as the trees thinned, I could see a wide, rocky river, swollen from the monsoon rains. The banks either side were steep and slippery. I didn't relish the thought of crossing this obstacle course one little bit!

'Ron.'

'Yeah?'

'I . . . er . . . I canna swim, Ron.'

He looked at the fast-flowing river then back at me and grinned. 'You poor bugger!'

Fortunately the officer in charge knew what he was doing. He was a good man to lead us, hardened and experienced by action in Malaya, yet thoughtful and considerate as long as you didn't put a foot wrong with him. 'Quiet, lads,' he said softly. 'Sergeant, post lookouts. We don't want to be picked off while we're crossing.' He then began to organise a human chain of well-built, strong-swimming soldiers, which included Mick and Eric, and sent them into the fast-flowing current. Holding their rifles over their heads and struggling to keep their balance, they were soon up to their armpits in the swollen waters. They linked arms, forming a human chain, then one by one the rest of the platoon slid down the embankment and proceeded to move from shoulder to shoulder across the river. Ronnie and I were among the last to cross.

Holding his rifle above his head Ronnie slid down the muddy embankment. I followed close on his heels, nervously scanning the water for snakes, crocodiles or any of the other unpleasantaries we'd been warned about. Within seconds the river was well above my waist and I was struggling to keep my balance, hold my rifle above my head, cling on to the human chain for support and at the same time keep an eye on the thick jungle either side of the river for Commie bandits figuring on using us for target practice. It was a great relief to see the bank ahead grow closer and feel the bed of the river rise. Thankfully I scrambled up the muddy slope after Ronnie and joined the rest of the platoon who were frantically stripping off their wet clothes and examining with horror the black slimy slugs clinging to their bodies.

'Leeches! Ugh, Ron, they're all over!' Shivering with repulsion I stripped off and with shaking hands we helped one another burn the leeches off our bodies with the tip of a cigarette. They shrivelled up and fell to the ground.

'Whatever you do, don't pull them off or you'll leave their heads in your skin and they'll poison you,' the officer cautioned. 'Then all of you check your kit. We'll establish a base here for the night and make an early start in the morning.'

Sentries were posted, and tommy cookers, water bottles and mess tins were produced as the platoon settled down for the evening using clumps of bushes for cover. With a sigh of relief I sank to the ground near Eric, laid out my ration tin then reached for my water bottle which was normally attached to my web belt. It was gone! Anxiously I glanced around, hoping I'd dropped it when we'd been burning off the leeches, but there was no sign of it. Frantically I began thrashing around in the undergrowth.

'Lost something, Annand?' the sergeant asked, coming up behind me.

'My water bottle, sergeant.'

He glared at me with contempt. 'Then I suggest you look for it in the obvious place, lad. The river! Otherwise you're gonna be dead from thirst before you get back to base!' As an afterthought he added, 'And should you manage to survive, Annand, you'll be on a charge. Losing government property is a serious offence!' He marched off to throw someone else into the pit of despair. He was a nasty piece of work, this particular sergeant.

Mick, Ronnie, Eric and one or two others joined in the search. If I'd lost it in the middle of the river then I was in trouble. A few minutes later a call from Mick brought us to rocks further down river where he'd been searching.

'I've found it, but I canna reach it from here. There it is. See? Wedged between those boulders.'

We stood in silence surveying the dark green water bottle at least five feet underwater. My heart sank. 'How'm I gonna get that?'

Eric eyed me cautiously. 'We could tip you upside down and lower you into the water.'

'No way!' I vehemently exploded, but after reflecting on the alternative of going thirsty and then being put on a charge which could result in anything from washing dishes, cleaning the cookhouse or toilets and being confined to barracks, I decided that, on balance, being tipped upside down into a leech-infested river was a far better prospect. 'OK then,' I reluctantly agreed. Stripping to the waist I took a deep breath, then Mick and Eric grasped my legs and lowered me into the fast-flowing current. As the roar of the river closed over me I thought enviously of George Brown, serving with the RAF near Leicester. I thrashed about in the water, afraid to open my eyes in case a leech landed on my eyeball or a snake gave me the once-over. My lungs were on the point of bursting before they hauled me up. I lay on the rock, gasping for breath.

'I think you need to be a bit lower and a fraction to your right, Alex,' Eric said, peering into the water. My stomach churned at the thought of going back into the river again, but several dippings later, just as I was becoming more confident, my hand grasped a familiar object and I was hauled out. Exhausted and coughing up river water, I flopped down on the bank clutching my water bottle. All desire for a drink had gone. I'd swallowed enough water to last me the rest of our journey. My head was swimming and there was a pain in my left ear.

Ronnie frowned at me. 'You've gone a funny colour. Kept you upside down too long, I think.'

I staggered to my feet and we made our way back to the rest of the platoon.

Throwing a couple of large branches in my direction he said 'You really don't look so good, Alex. Better get yourself ready for bed before it gets dark.'

Feeling semi-drunk, I erected a frame from the branches, the way we'd been trained and threw my cape over the top, making a bivouac. Then I changed into dry clothes, crawled inside my bed roll and lay shivering.

Mick lifted the edge of the cape. 'You OK, Alex?' There was a note of concern in his voice.

'Yes . . . yes. I'm OK,' I said through chattering teeth.

'Ron says you look awful and you've had no dinner. You'll be starving.'

'No, I'm not hungry. I just want to sleep. I'll be fine in the morning.'

He nodded and left me alone.

Sounds from outside my bivouac drifted in. Laughter from the platoon, the hiss of Primus stoves and the smell of baked beans, brewed tea and soup. I pulled my clothes around me for warmth and closed my eyes. The laughter moved to a gentle hum of conversation and the jungle noises grew quieter as darkness descended upon the camp.

I fell into a delirious sleep, waking frequently throughout the night with an excruciating earache, the like of which I'd never experienced since childhood. I felt hot and sticky and was aware that I was quietly moaning. Eventually I must have fallen into a deep sleep, for when I awoke the sun was filtering through the trees, bringing the jungle to life. There were stirrings from the platoon and a blessed relief from the pain in my ear. I moved my head cautiously and felt something trickle down the side of my face. I touched it gingerly. It was warm and sticky. I sat up to look at my fingers and the ground swam before me. Sluggishly I crawled out of my bivouac to the Primus stove with one thought on my mind. A cup of tea. I'd feel better after a cup of tea. Mick looked up from where he and Eric were sitting having breakfast. 'Good grief! What's up wi'y' ear, Alex? It's a mess.'

'It's OK.' My voice sounded far away.

'What d' you mean "OK"? It's pouring wi' blood.'

I touched my ear, then looked stupidly at my blood-soaked fingers. A mug of tea was thrust into my hands. 'Here, try this,' someone said. It was hot and sweet.

The medical orderly appeared on the scene and began asking questions. I could hear my voice slurring as I answered him. He fed me pills and breakfast, then bathed my ear while soldiers moved around like ants in an artificial world as they broke camp. I had a zany desire to laugh but wasn't too sure what the joke was.

The sergeant came to see me, then the officer and eventually, after much debate between them, I was hauled to my feet and with support from some of my mates, I followed the platoon like a zombie through the thick jungle towards our evening rendezvous with the lorries. By midday the humidity of the jungle had increased my temperature and I was soaked in a hot sweat. The concerned faces of my mates and the medical orderly swam in front of me each time we made a stop, which was more frequent than usual to allow me to rest. I kept falling to the ground and entering the colourful delirious world of senseless nightmares and dreams, waking up with the sweat running down my body, my head pounding and my stomach retching. Eventually I reached the point where I honestly wanted to die.

It must have been late afternoon before I started coming to my senses. 'I'm thirsty,' I said. My voice sounded thick and guttural.

Ronnie handed me his water bottle and with shaking hands I pressed it to my lips. Cold water trickling down the back of my parched throat never tasted so good. I poured it over my head and neck. It was heaven. Slowly the world seemed to be returning to normal.

'You look better,' Ronnie said with a broad grin. 'Well, you don't look as bad, anyhow.'

The sergeant came up to the rear of the column. 'How you feeling, lad?' he said. Surprisingly he seemed genuinely concerned.

'Still a bit queasy and feverish, sergeant, but a bit better.'

'OK. Take it easy. Not far to the clearing now. Hopefully the lorries will be there ahead of us.'

About half an hour later it dawned on me that we seemed to be following a set track and leaving the density of the forest behind us. Eventually the officer lifted his hand and we stopped, closing ranks behind him. He signalled his instructions to check the area, and we silently crept forward. There was no sign of the trucks. Cautiously we entered the clearing.

'All clear!' the sergeant barked in a loud whisper. 'You and you!' he pointed to two tired soldiers. 'Sentry duty. Keep your eyes peeled! Right!'

The platoon settled down uneasily to wait for the transport, sprawled out around the clearing and side of the track, trying to catch the last of the daylight filtering through the crown of leaves. Wearily I drifted over to a log with Ronnie, Mick and Eric and with moans of relief we dropped our armoury and haversacks on the ground.

Mick pulled out his ration tin. 'You'd better have a bite to eat, Alex, keep your strength up.' I peered inside at the meagre remains of food and forced myself to eat the few crumbly biscuits and his last square of chocolate.

'I thought we were here to fight Commies, not flaming mosquitoes,' Ronnie said, slapping the back of his neck.

'You'll find the enemy soon enough,' the sergeant said threateningly. 'And just so as we're always on the ready, lads . . .' he raised his voice so that the whole platoon knew his next comment was addressed to all of us, ' . . . let's see if we can have your weapons sparkling like the crown jewels while we wait for our transport.'

There was a low rumble of groans as footsore, weary soldiers complained at having these few precious moments of rest denied them. Ronnie, sitting straddled across a log, rested his Bren gun in front of him. 'As if I'm not knackered enough carrying half of Alex's gear, now it's cleaning firearms! The army never lets you alone for five bloody minutes.'

Although exhausted after the events of the previous evening and the day-long march through the hot jungle, I was now less delirious and even felt able to cope with the well-rehearsed procedure of removing the magazine case and cleaning the gun. I sat on the log beside Ronnie and spat on a lump of brown earth caked to the barrel of my gun then rubbed rigorously. The rest of the platoon were quietly cleaning their firearms, enjoying the peace and quiet of the evening after the heavy heat of the day. I glanced up sharply as something rustled in the undergrowth but it was only the sound of the jungle settling down for the evening. The sun flickered through the fronds of bamboo which had formed a neat lacework pattern in the trees above. Gradually its gentle warmth enveloped me and before long my eyelids developed lead weights. I leant back against a branch, realising how exhausted I was after the ordeal of the last twenty-four hours. Slowly the welcome blanket of sleep began to creep over me, warming, soothing . . .

Rat! Tat! tat! Tat! Tat! . . . The sharp crack of an automatic weapon sliced through the evening air, sending birds screeching from the trees. In that split second, from the first round of machine-gun fire, I had thrown myself backwards off the log and lay flat and shaking under its meagre cover.

'Oh, God help us!' I muttered, breaking out into a cold sweat. 'We're under attack!' I rolled over to grab my rifle, still under cover of the log and to my horror realised I had left it half-assembled. Gingerly I reached up for the magazine case, peering around the clearing as I did so. Amazingly our well-trained platoon had disappeared behind trees or into the undergrowth. The clearing was deserted. Deserted that is, except for one solitary figure. Ronnie Palmer! He sat on the log like a marble statue with his mouth wide open, his Bren gun pointing to the sky with wisps of smoke still coming from the barrel and his finger frozen on the trigger.

The officer was the first to break our cover. He strode over towards Ronnie, his face contorted with rage. The sergeant was hard on his heels. For once Ronnie was lost for words. The officer wasn't!

'You great steaming nit, Palmer!' he bellowed. 'Three of my lads back there have filled their pants because of your . . . your bloody stupidity! I'll have you court-martialled for this!'

The sergeant added his ten penneth. 'You'll get the book thrown at you for this, you ****! Call yourself a soldier? You stupid ****!'

Fortunately the heavy groaning of labouring engines brought the tirade to an end.

'Sort you out later, Palmer!' he concluded.

The rest of the platoon broke cover and watched as the trucks struggled up the track lurching from side to side. After three days in the raw Malayan jungle they were a welcome sight. Thankfully and wearily we clambered on board for a bone-shaking journey back to our camp at Kluang.

'You could've killed the lot o' us, Ron!' one of the lads exploded as our lorry got under way.

'Aye. It's a court martial offence and you bloody well deserve it!' another one snarled.

'I know! I know! Shut up!' Ronnie snapped. His face was as white as a sheet and he was obviously embarrassed by his carelessness.

'Don't worry, Ron. It was an accident.' Mick gave him a friendly grin.

'Try telling that to them!' Ronnie indicated the truck in front carrying the officer and sergeant.

'No one was hurt. The CO'll take that into consideration.'

Ronnie shook his head. 'Reckon it's the glasshouse for me. If ever I needed a prayer, Mick, it's now. Say one for me, eh?'

Mick nodded. 'OK mate,' he said quietly. 'Consider it done.'

Ronnie sat morose and silent for the rest of the journey.

It was dark when we arrived back at Kluang. The officer and sergeant climbed wearily out of their trucks.

'Everyone out! Weapons to the armoury! Hot shower and meals,' the sergeant bellowed. Then he turned towards Ronnie. 'Palmer! Come here!'

The platoon headed for their huts with a few backward glances in Ronnie's direction but I think most of them felt he deserved what he was going to get.

Despite still feeling weak and a bit nauseous, I stood with Mick and Eric in the dimly-lit compound. We were reluctant to leave our mate, who no doubt faced a night in the guardhouse before charges were brought against him.

Night brought with it a welcome coolness to the air. The surrounding jungle was quiet except for the occasional screech or roar of a disturbed animal. I thought longingly of the warm shower to wash away the sweat and dirt of the last few days, the cooked dinner with meat and vegetables and the privacy of my comfortable bed under its mosquito net, but I couldn't seem to pull myself away from the huddle of officers and the sergeant standing with Ronnie by one of the administration huts. A few minutes later the huddle broke up and Ronnie made his way over to where we were standing.

'Well?'

His cheeky grin was back. 'I can't believe it! God Almighty! I would never have believed he could do it!'

Mick glowered at him. It was the first time a blasphemy had passed Ronnie's lips since he'd had the brush with Mick.

'No! No! I mean he, God Almighty.' He pointed to the stars. 'I would never have believed he could do it, but he must have! There's no other explanation!' Ronnie was obviously elated over something or other.

'What are you talking about?'

'He must have heard your prayer, Mick. Why else would they say, "Forget the whole incident." That's what they said. Honest to God, just like that. "Forget the whole incident." '

'You're joking!'

'No! I swear!' Ronnie shrugged. 'There was a lot of "There'll be no second chance" and "Watch it from now on, Palmer" but in the end they've decided to hush the whole thing up. Can you believe it?' He shook his head as if trying to make sense of the situation himself. Then he said, 'Howay, lads! I'm starving, sweaty and I'm dying for a shower!' Obviously very relieved, he jauntily led the way up the terraces to our hut with Eric on his heels.

As I made to follow him into the darkness I spotted a wide smile on Mick's face.

'So, er . . . did you pray?' I asked him.

'Aye,' he said quietly.

As I made my way up the terraces I didn't for one minute believe Ronnie's reprieve had been an answer to prayer. Things like that didn't happen, but once again I couldn't help but wonder about this God of Mick's who could draw even a hardened character like Ronnie into believing in him.

As I fell into an exhausted sleep that night the question that kept reverberating around my head was 'Could it have been an answer to prayer?'

∞ 9 ∞

'Hello? Hello? Kampong Hospital? It's the Medical Officer from army barracks Kluang here. Sorry to ring you at this early hour of the morning but one of our lads. pardon? . . . I said KLUANG! I know it's a terrible line. Our lads have been on jungle patrol and one of them has returned with an ear . . . JUNGLE PATROL!' The MO looked across to where I sat and raised his eyebrows despairingly. 'The sooner they get the communications in this part of the country sorted . . . yes . . . hello? It's his ear. No. No. EAR. It probably just needs a shot of penicillin but I think you'd better . . . I said a SHOT OF . . . yes . . . OK . . . fine. I'll get him to you as quickly as possible. Thank you.' With a sigh of relief he replaced the receiver and turned to me. 'OK, Annand. I'm sure it's nothing more than a bad infection but we need to be certain. I'm sending you to Kampong Hospital, they'll sort you out. Keep that pad on your ear, it'll help stem the flow of blood.

'Yes, sir.' Shakily I stood up and the infirmary turned upside down.

Although I'd showered and had my ear cleaned up after our return to Kluang camp, I'd had very little to eat and my temperature had soared again through the night. My delirious cries had woken the whole hut so Eric had thought it advisable to take me to the MO's surgery where I now sat, fully dressed, still a bit non compos mentis and with my ear more painful than ever.

Eric steadied me until I'd regained my balance then helped me to the compound where he strapped me on to the stretcher at the back of his jeep. I was more comfortable lying down. The medical orderly, Jim, sat beside me and Eric jumped into the driver's seat. Then, escorted by an armoured truck, we drove at speed through the early morning jungle to the army hospital at Kampong, a few miles away. During the night it had rained steadily, leaving ditches and potholes in the road swimming with water. A light breeze sprang up as we drove, catching the giant leaves overhead and sending a steady shower on to our jeep. Daybreak arrived swiftly as we entered Kampong, bringing with it a dull grey sky which mercifully kept the mosquitoes at bay.

We pulled up at the hospital gates expecting to have our identifications checked but to our surprise we were waved straight through, and to our greater surprise we were met at the main doors of the hospital by a medical theatre team all fully gowned and masked.

'Get this man to surgery quickly!' One of the doctors motioned to an orderly standing by with a trolley. I saw Eric and Jim glance at each other in alarm then Jim stepped forward. 'I'm the medical orderly from Kluang camp. I think . . .'

'Yes. We know who you are,' one of the doctors interrupted. 'Your Medical Officer rang earlier.'

The hospital team had already unstrapped me, hoisted me on to the trolley and then began pushing me through the doors of the hospital with such a sense of urgency that even I, in my delirious state, was surprised.

'Tell Dr Richards the emergency from Kluang has arrived!' one of the nurses called. 'We're taking him to theatre two!'

'Emergency!' I slurred, trying to sit up. 'What emergency?'

'Sir . . .' my medical orderly panted as he ran through the corridors alongside my trolley. 'Sir, I don't think . . .'

I never found out what he thought. I was pushed firmly back into a lying position, whisked into the operating theatre and he and Eric had the doors firmly closed in their faces.

A tall, gowned, masked and gloved doctor and his anaesthetist stood waiting. 'You're the young man who was shot in the ear, I take it? Nothing to worry about, son. We'll soon have the bullet out.'

I wasn't THAT non compos mentis! 'SHOT IN THE EAR? No! I haven't been shot!' I cried in panic. 'You've got it wrong. I've got an ear infection, that's all!'

Doctors and nurses eyed each other uncertainly over their masks.

'It's true!' I shouted, struggling to sit up. 'Ask my medical orderly!'

There was more eyeing over masks, then a lot of toing and froing before Jim was brought in and a thorough examination of my ear took place. No bullet was found. The doctor furiously whipped off his mask. 'We're rushed off our feet here, soldier! My staff have hardly slept for three days and have worked overtime getting the theatre scrubbed up and ready for you! On top of that, I was called in, on my day off, expecting to find an emergency and instead find you lying here with . . . with an ear-ache!'

'It's not my fault I wasn't shot!' I spluttered. 'I've done nothing wrong!'

'Except waste everybody's time, create havoc from the main gate through to theatre and ruin the first English breakfast I've had in three months!' He stripped off his gown and gloves in disgust and stormed out.

As the hubbub of excitement died down I struggled to fight off the sudden waves of nausea which had crept up on me due to lack of sleep, hunger and the chaos of the last few hours. I closed my eyes, listening to the medical staff give their varied opinions on the state of health they'd like to see me in as they left the theatre, then silence descended and I was left alone.

An aroma of sweet perfume suddenly wafted around the trolley where I lay. I opened one eye and through blurred vision made out the shapely form of a nurse in a low-cut starched white uniform. Long strands of blonde wavy hair struggled to escape from under her cap. 'Let's get those pants off, soldier,' she said in a sultry voice. I grinned deliriously at her. 'Hang on, nurse. Don't rush me. I don't even know your name yet!'

She chuckled. 'You're a lucky lad,' she said, pulling my boots off.

'Lucky?'

She unfastened my trousers. 'Yes. The message we got from Kluang said you'd been shot in the ear. They were just about to open you up for major surgery.' She pulled my trousers off. 'Seems as though we could do with operating on the telephone system in this country before anything else.'

'So what are they going to do with me? Or more importantly, what are you going to do with me, nurse?'

She smiled and rolled me over. She really was an extremely warm, attractive . . . 'Doctor thinks a shot of penicillin should do the trick and as for me, I'm going to give you your first shot now.'

I groaned and lay with my head between my arms trying to curb the vivid memories from childhood of needles, medicines and smells of antiseptic. 'I hate needles!' I muttered. 'I hate hospitals. I don't want to be given an injection.'

'No, no. We're not going to give you an injection,' she soothed, slapping something cold, wet and smelling suspiciously like antiseptic on my bottom. 'You're going to give yourself one.'

I raised my head, slightly confused, and the theatre swam around me. 'How can I give myself . . .?' The resounding smack on my bottom gave me such a shock that my rear jerked into the air towards and into the point of the needle. 'Aahhh!'

'Bull's-eye!' my mentor chortled. 'All done.' With a friendly pat on the buttocks I watched a pair of shapely legs in white stockings glide out of the theatre, leaving me in a state of undress, humiliation and with a pain in my rear end to add to all my other ailments.

The Medical Officer was right. It was just a bad infection and a few days in hospital soon put it right. Still weak but at least free from pain, I returned to Kluang on light duties which meant, much to my relief, that I was excluded from jungle patrol.

When I'd first arrived in Singapore I'd been made batman to a Captain Wainwright and as he was leaving to see his family for a long overdue vacation in Singapore, he suggested I take a few days' leave for convalescing and travel back with him. This was the best idea the army had ever come up with!

It was good to be back in Singapore again, to walk on clean paved streets, admire the colourful sarongs of the Malay women or to loiter over a meal of curry and rice washed down with Tiger beer. Sometimes I'd meander around the major shops and stores or down the side alleys and markets where the hustle and bustle of merchants vied for trade and the inevitable watch salesmen lurked around corners: 'Psst! Wanna buy a watch?' Around these side alleys and markets children of eight or nine pestered for money and pulled at your shirt sleeve. 'Hey, Jonnie. You want my sister?' and a young prostitute, barely in her teens, hovered in the background. It was a world far removed from the jungles of Malaya. However, after a few days of sightseeing on my own I grew increasingly lonely and waves of self-pity engulfed me as I realised it was taking longer for me to recover than I'd imagined. I hated being sick.

I was down at the harbour one day watching a flotilla of boats and ships of all sizes and descriptions docking or setting sail, when a young man, enthusiastically selling medicinal herbs, roots and potions drew my attention by the huge crowd he was gathering around him. Suddenly a familiar accent caught my attention.

'Och, man, Harry. You canna go asking these furreners where Sentosa Island is. We need to find a map or see if there's someone in that crowd who speaks English or summat.'

'How about a Jock from Aberdeen like yourself?' I interjected, grinning.

Three sailors turned to me with amazed expressions. 'Aberdeen? You're from Aberdeen?' one of them asked with a beaming smile.

'Aye. Alex Annand with the 1st Battalion East Yorkshire Regiment.'

For the next hour and a half I was lost to the world as I chatted with my fellow countrymen and before I knew it we'd made plans to go sightseeing. The British Fleet had landed and they didn't want to miss a thing that Singapore had to offer.

The flurry of sightseeing, meals, drinks and night clubs wasn't quite the way I was meant to convalesce. My head hardly touched the pillow for the next few nights and my consumption of Tiger beer served to act as a painkiller, antibiotic and memory block all rolled into one.

On the second, third (or was it the fourth?) day, we started celebrating at the Raffles Hotel, sipping tea served by immaculately white-clad waiters. After a few hours we were supping beer in one of the many nightclubs Singapore has to offer. What we were celebrating I'm not quite sure, not that it mattered. This was my last evening with my fellow countrymen before returning to Kluang so it warranted a celebration. It was a good night – I think – and after a loud and boisterous farewell I left my companions to return to the hostel sometime after – well, I can't remember that, either!

The bright lights of the city swung furiously to and fro in the dark night air. Traffic thundered past and the streets were filled with tourists, British forces and locals enjoying a night on the town. The smell of curry drifted past, reminding me I ought to eat. I couldn't remember when I'd had my last meal but my stomach told me one was about due. For the last few days I'd been almost continually in the company of my Scottish companions, eating, sleeping, sightseeing and drinking with them and now, wandering through the streets on my own, I felt surprisingly lonely again. Their constant companionship, exchanging news from home in my own native tongue, telling jokes and sampling the delights of Singapore had sadly come to an end. I glanced around me. I was well away from the main streets now and my hostel was just across the road.

I stepped off the pavement, turned and was just in time to see a large grey bus bearing down on me. As if in slow motion I watched the driver's face contort with horror as he saw me lurch in front of his bus. His hands tightened on the steering wheel, his body stiffened as he rammed his foot on the brakes and the blast of his horn and screech of tyres pulsated through my painful ear. In that split, panic-stricken second I knew escape was futile. It wouldn't be a bullet that got me but . . . Suddenly a large hand grasped me firmly by the shoulder, hauling me out of the path of the oncoming bus with such force that I lost my balance and sprawled on all fours across the pavement. The bus thundered past with the driver's fist waving angrily in my direction.

I lay stunned and winded, trying to catch my breath, then gratefully looked round to thank my rescuer. There was no one there. A young Chinese couple stood smooching in a nearby doorway. A small elderly Malayan gentleman, some twenty to thirty yards away, shuffled slowly towards me with the aid of a stick. In the distance a well-built man in shorts walked briskly in the opposite direction, but it was impossible to tell whether he was Asian or European as he never once glanced back. I stood up, shaking but completely sober. Two small shabby, bronzed children of about six or seven watched me curiously with wide brown eyes.

'Did that man pull me away from . . ?' I pointed to the receding figure of the man in shorts then realised the children couldn't understand a word I was saying. I dropped my arm then slowly and thoughtfully made my way over to the hostel where I spent the next few hours hanging over the lavatory pan, pledging abstinence from alcohol for the rest of my life.

That night, as I lay in bed, I could still feel the powerful grip on my shoulder that had hurled me out of the path of the bus and saved my life. But who was it that had been my guardian angel? Why didn't he stop? Why didn't he look back? Why had he hurried away? I could find no explanation, but I was extremely glad to be alive!

℃ℛ 10 ℬℴ

A few weeks later the whole regiment was pulled out of Kluang and ordered to return to Singapore to support the troops in Selerang Garrison. Not surprisingly the political unrest in the country had caused riots in the streets of Singapore and the normally controlled temperament of the people had exploded in exasperation. As we journeyed back across the causeway we were disturbed to see for ourselves the carnage left by the rioters. Grim-faced shopkeepers attempted to replace smashed windows and restore order to their damaged premises. Litter and rubbish filled the streets and an upturned car which had been set alight still smouldered, leaving a pungnent smell of petrol in the air.

It was only as we drew closer to Selerang Garrison that we met with trouble ourselves. A large group of local men, women and youths armed with machetes, sticks and stones blocked our route. Our convoy came to a grinding halt, all too aware that we were sitting targets. Hot and tired from our long overnight journey we were in no mood to face this unexpected aggression.

Both groups eyed each other warily: the rioters not wishing to take on the armed might of the British Army and our convoy not wishing to incite an ugly incident. 'Fix bayonets and keep it quiet, lads, we're going straight through.' The calm reassuring voice of the sergeant carried from the front of the column. Silently we fixed our bayonets. Our lorry revved its engine and the convoy moved slowly forward, parting the rioters. Suddenly a war cry shrilled from the group and a stone hurtled through the air, hitting the side of our truck. It was quickly followed by a barrage of sticks, bottles and rotten fruit and vegetables.

'Keep your heads down!' bellowed the sergeant.

'Stupid ****. What's he expect us to do?' I swore, wiping something red and foul-smelling from my shoulder.

The truck started to pick up speed but the rioters ran after us. Turning the corner we were relieved to see Selerang Garrison come into view. Our attackers hesitated. The ringleaders lost their nerve and one by one they melted back into the streets and alley-ways. With a sigh of relief we picked up speed and drove rapidly through the barrack gates, ourselves and the trucks covered in rotten vegetables.

We didn't realise until later that we'd been deliberately driven through the streets of Singapore as a show of strength. Martial law had been declared, a strict curfew imposed and now our training was for a different type of warfare: that of dealing with civil unrest.

In the sweltering tropical heat of the parade ground we paraded, day after day, for hours on end in steel helmets, full pack and fixed bayonets. No explanations. We did as we were told. Soldiers on parade dropped like flies as the heat became too much for them. We soon discovered we weren't the only troops called back into Singapore. A company of Gurkhas arrived.

'Look,' Eric prodded me with his boot as we took one of the rare moments in the day for a rest.

I sat up. 'They're tiny,' I observed.

'Aye, but tough jungle fighters.' Ronnie shaded his eyes to watch them assemble for drill. 'I've heard that with one swoop of that cookery knife of theirs they can cut your head off.'

'Ugh! You're kidding.'

'Rumour has it that if they pull their knife they won't return it without blood on it! They say they're one of the few foes the Japanese feared during the last war. The Commie bandits are terrified of them.'

Mick shaded his eyes. 'Good job they're on our side, then.'

We discovered this smart, efficient fighting force to be a friendly, cheerful bunch with a great sense of humour but, though they were friendly towards us, they kept themselves very much to themselves.

Training took quite an interesting slant shortly after that. Half the regiment were ordered to dress up as civilian rioters and attack the other half dressed in full military gear.

'No holds barred; give 'em what for,' the sergeant barked.

Standing in a colourful shirt, a pair of red shorts, a headband and brandishing a stick I was raring to have a go at him.

'Make it as realistic as possible!' he bellowed. 'Only remember, you buggers, you're back in uniform when this is over, so touch me if you dare!'

After eight weeks of being tied to barracks these war games became a source of release and we threw ourselves wholeheartedly into them despite the cuts and bruises we received. Completely out of the blue and much to everyone's surprise the riots in Singapore ended as quickly as they'd started and we were allowed to spend our leave in the city. We didn't question the speed with which order had been restored; we just accepted it, glad to have avoided action. With the regiment due to return home to the UK in a few weeks, our thoughts turned to presents for our families and how we could have a last fling in the city.

Sunday morning found me in a foul mood. There was nothing really strange about that. I'd always hated Sundays since being a kid. The closed shops, nothing to do and the pressure of being made to go to church. The army, I discovered, didn't change any of that but, for some reason, this Sunday I'd had enough and was damned if I was going to be marched off to church and forced into worship!

'I can't go, sergeant,' I said. 'It's against my religion.'

'Oh? And what religion is that, Annand?'

'Church of Scotland, sergeant.'

'I see. A Church of Scotland service forbids you to go to a Church of England service, does it? How come these religious principles have never bothered you before?'

I shrugged non-committally.

'I know your game, Annand, and it won't wash with me. You can refuse to go to church but not church parade. I want to see you on the parade ground with the rest of the regiment. Clear?'

'Yes, sergeant. Er . . . sergeant?'

'Yes, Annand, what now?'

'You said I could refuse to go to church but not church parade. Is that right?'

His eyes glinted warningly. 'Yes, soldier.'

'Well, I'll do that then. I'll go to the parade and miss the service.'

The rebellion against the battalion church service certainly wasn't winning me any Brownie points. The sergeant took a deep breath and snarled, 'On the parade ground 11.00 hours. Right?'

'Right, sergeant.'

As soon as he'd left the dormitory I flung myself on the bed. I didn't like to be told 'You have to go to church.' Church didn't spell good news for me. Sunday school had been a series of disasters. In fact I would have been the first pupil to be expelled for misbehaviour if the minister hadn't stepped in. He hadn't done me any favours either with the discipline he'd enforced. The only pleasant memories I had of Sunday school were the pranks Jimmy and I had played on the long-suffering teachers, the girls we'd met and the fights I'd won. My adult opinion of church was that its only use was to give people a good set of principles to live by. The regimental face-ache we had as a chaplain hadn't done anything to change my views either. He was an officer, intent on duty and loyalty to the army and that was what he preached, in a manner that made darned sure you wouldn't forget them.

'Hey, Alex man. What's up wi' your face? It's tripping you!' Ronnie wandered up to my bed.

'Nowt!'

'You're not still whingeing on about that blinking church service, are you? Did you try the one on being Church of Scotland?'

'Aye. I tried. I think I'm let off going to the service, but I've gotta go to the parade.'

'That's not so bad, then.'

'Suppose not.'

'For heaven's sake smile, then! It's not like you to look so sour, and God knows we could do with a bit of light relief if we've gotta go to church.'

He was right, of course. It was ridiculous to let this church thing get out of hand. But later that day, as we marched to the service, my rebellion rose to a new height.

'Annand!' the sergeant barked as we reached the entrance to the field where the service was to be held. I could see the whole battalion prick up its ears. 'Haven't you claimed exemption from the church service on the grounds you belong to the Church of Scotland?'

I could feel my face turning scarlet at the stifled snorts of mirth around me. 'Yes, sir.'

'Then we'll leave you here by this gate then, soldier.'

Humiliated and furious, I watched the regiment march to the field where every hymn, prayer, Bible reading and every word of the sermon was transmitted into a microphone, making the whole service clearly audible from my position by the gate. I stood with the blistering heat penetrating through my uniform, longing to sit down but not daring to since I had been ordered to remain standing at ease, still on parade.

Eventually the service came to an end and Captain Wainwright wandered over to where I stood. With a wry smile and a touch of warmth in his voice he said, 'When will you learn, Annand? You can't beat the army and if you can't beat them, you might as well join them. It makes life so much easier in the end. You really are a very stubborn man.' Shaking his head despairingly he wandered off to talk to another officer.

As everyone took their places for the march back to the barracks, I saw the sergeant talking to the chaplain, who nodded, raised his eyebrows then looked pointedly in my direction. A slow smile crossed his face, then he and the sergeant burst out laughing and it seemed to be at me. Whether or not that was true I would never know, but from that moment on I took an intense dislike towards army chaplaincy and anything to do with church, and decided that never again would they get the opportunity to embarrass me in this way.

Once back in the barracks I furiously hurled my cap and belt in the corner and myself on the bed.

Eric eyed me warily. 'Come on, Alex. Don't you think you're carrying this thing about church a bit far?'

'Shut it!'

'Howay, Alex man.' Ronnie sat on the bottom of the bed. 'Let's go for a beer.'

'I said shut it!' I snarled.

He shrugged and he and Eric headed off to the NAAFI. Mick wisely ignored me as he lay on his bed pretending to read.

'Aye well, if you ask me it serves you right, Jock. You going around so bloody cheerful in this heat was getting right on my wick!' The speaker was a large, thickset, hard lad. I hadn't had many dealings with him. I think he disliked me as much as I did him, although there was no real reason for this.

'Get off my back, Murchie!'

'Riled, are we?' he smirked. 'What's the matter? Lost your sense of humour at having to stand all through the . . .' He took a step back as I angrily leapt off my bed.

'I said lay off, Murchie!'

'If you could have seen yourself. You looked like . . .'

Furiously I hurled myself in his direction and, despite being half his size, threw a weighty punch at his jaw. He ducked, laughing as I crashed to the floor. Still laughing he towered over me, then, reaching down, grabbed me by the collar of my uniform and hauled me to my feet. Before I'd had a chance to gather my wits about me his right fist shot out towards me. I heard a crunch, felt a stabbing pain to my jaw and watched, surprised, as a spurt of blood shot over his uniform. Out of the corner of my eye I saw Mick leap off his bed just as Murchie's fist was about to deliver a second blow.

'That's enough! That's enough!' Mick grabbed his arm and swung him round so they were face to face. 'That's enough! OK, Murchie?'

Murchinson hesitated. He had no wish to argue with Mick. Fortunately a couple of his own mates arrived on the scene, grabbed his arms and after a bit of gentle persuasion, attempted to drag him out of the room. He threw some verbal abuse in my direction before disappearing out of the door but had obviously decided to let the matter drop.

'What's up wi'y', Alex?' Mick said, sitting on the floor beside me. 'You're acting like a lunatic! It was only a church service, after all!'

I put my head between my hands and leant back against the wall. 'I dunno, Mick.' That spurt of aggression against Murchie seemed to have knocked all the fight out of me. 'What the hell's it all about, Mick? I'm damned if I know.'

He didn't answer. He got to his feet, collected my flannel, ran it under the cold tap then came back and handed it to me. I dabbed it on my split lip.

'Ouch!' I transferred it to my swelling eyebrow and groaned with pain. After a moment I said, 'Can I ask you something, Mick?'

'Aye.' He sat down on the chair beside my bed. We had the room to ourselves.

'Why is religion and church so important to you?'

'They're not.'

I looked up at him, surprised, and he grinned. 'They're not,' he repeated. 'But Jesus is.' He stretched back in the chair, put his feet on my bed and his arms behind his head. 'Eric and some of the married lads tell us how they met their wives. Some of them in pubs, a dance or social. My story's not much different. I met Jesus in a pub.'

'A pub?'

'Aye, a pub. Me and some of the lads were on a pub crawl. I was half-cut at the time and we decided it would be a good laugh to go to Prudhoe Mission and cause some trouble.'

I stared at him, amazed. This didn't sound like the Mick I knew. 'You're having me on!'

'No. Honest. We barged in expecting to find hostile Holy Joes bellowing at us to get out, but this geezer at the front says, "Howay in, lads. You're welcome." '

There was a silence. 'Is that it?'

'More or less. Next thing I knew they'd invited us to stay for tea. So we did, just for a lark, but there was something about this old geezer's word of welcome that stuck with me. How come this group of Holy Joes wanted me? Me! In my hostile drunken state. The following night we went drinking again and once more ended up at the Mission for a laugh. They'll soon get sick of us, call the cops we thought. But they didn't.' Mick shrugged. 'Dunno why they put up with me and the lads, but they did. Then I started asking questions, cursing them, arguing with them about their beliefs but still they didn't call the cops. A couple of weeks later we were out on a pub crawl when suddenly, sitting in the corner of the pub, waiting for my third pint, I heard God speak to me. He said, "Let me be part of your life, Mick." '

I shuffled uncomfortably, embarrassed by the familiarity of his relationship with this God of his whom he claimed spoke to him. Of course, I'd met people before who'd claimed God spoke to them but on the rare occasions I'd talked to God, he'd never replied or appeared interested enough to talk to me.

'That's it, really,' Mick concluded. There was an awkward silence between us for a moment before he said, 'Fancy a beer, Alex?'

'Aye.'

'Right! Ronnie and Eric are in the NAAFI. Might as well join them. Make the most of our last few days in Singapore.'

'Aye.'

As we made our way over to the mess, Mick chatted easily about our return home but I was only half listening. The Sunday school, the youth club, the army services: these were all things of God, but they seemed a world far removed from the things Mick believed in. His God was real! Mick, this giant of a man, solid, fit, intelligent, who when riled could really explode but who most of the time was as gentle as a lamb, had a very special relationship going for him with his God – and I was envious!

A chill wind whipped around the corner of the brightly-lit dancehall, blowing gusts of sleet through my new lightweight summer suit, the last word in fashion from Singapore. Bronzed from my time in the Far East, I was conceited enough to know I looked good and cocky enough to revel in the admiring glances from the girls at the dance, but somehow the dashing image of the bronzed god was rapidly fading as the sleet soaked through the suit leaving me with a hangdog appearance. January weather on the north-east coast of England hadn't changed any, I noted, stamping my feet to keep warm. George, huddled in a nearby doorway saying goodnight to his girlfriend, could have been in the North Pole for all he cared.

'Come on, George, let the poor lass up for air and say goodnight. I'm frozen!' I complained, thrusting my cold hands into my trouser pockets. Thankfully her bus pulled up at the kerb just at that moment, sending a spray of slush over my canvas shoes. Icy water soaked through to my feet. After a final kiss, George's girlfriend leapt nimbly on board and we waved as the bus moved away. George fell into step beside me.

'Great night, eh, Alex?' Our feet made sloshing noises in the wet snow.

'You bet! I've got a date next week with that blonde lass. Whoops!' I slipped on the pavement and we walked in silence for a while, carefully avoiding the icy patches.

'Have you decided what you're going to do after demob in the spring?' George asked.

'What I'm going to do,' I repeated. That was the six million dollar question. My original idea had been to return to Aberdeen, but financially I didn't see how that would be possible.

'I suppose you'll be going back to Burton's?'

'Mmm.' The prospect of returning to work in a shop held little appeal for me.

Since I'd met up with George again we'd had this conversation a number of times, both of us aware that following demob we were likely to feel unsettled. It was a common experience for thousands of National Servicemen. I sighed. 'There must be more to life than going back to work in a shop, George.'

'Aye. There must be.' He pondered for a moment. 'Tell you what. My dad happens to be secretary of the Miner's Institute and he was telling me that the committee are after someone to help run a boy's club in the evenings. It's just a thought, but how about you and me giving it a go?'

Happy memories of the youth club at Aberdeen flooded into my mind. 'Mmm. Might be interesting.'

A week later we sat nervously in front of a small group of sombre, square-faced committee members who seemed less than interested in my wonderfully exaggerated achievements in the youth club in Aberdeen and even less interested in my valiant army ventures but more concerned about which professional football team we supported and the quality of our football coaching skills. I think they were pretty impressed by my further gross exaggerations because to our delight they employed us on the spot. George and I threw ourselves wholeheartedly into our new role which mainly consisted of being football coaches. Football, it seemed was the lads' primary activity. We were soon entering into league matches and even winning a few games. It was unfortunate, however, that after a few months the committee didn't see eye to eye with George and me. The problem was that we wanted to give all the enthusiastic lads a chance to play whereas the committee was more concerned with results and insisted on choosing the better players. Consequently there were continual disagreements until once again I let my mouth run away with me and told them what they could do with their football team. But by then I'd discovered I had a potential for organising boys' club activities, taking them camping and helping them in their Duke of Edinburgh Award Training Scheme. I had something to offer the lads and thoroughly enjoyed the physical activities that I'd missed in my own childhood. Ray Gray, an experienced club leader twenty years my senior, encouraged me to take a training course and then challenged me to start a youth club. With only twenty lads and œ5, I threw myself wholeheartedly into the challenge. Before long the membership had increased to one hundred and we had a nice healthy bank balance. This, I decided, was what I wanted to do with my spare time. I also decided to wave cheerio to Burton's after acquiring a job in the offices of the AA. The Automobile Association, not Alcoholics Anonymous.

One evening I was a bit perturbed to find the local policeman standing at the youth club door as I came to open up.

'Can I have a word in private, Alex?'

'Aye. Come on in. We'll go through to the back.'

He helped me to set up the pool table then followed me into the office. 'It's about young Jimmy,' he said. 'He's due to go to court for stealing.'

'Stealing!' I was horrified. 'I know he's a bit of a tearaway, but stealing?'

The policeman nodded. 'He's got quite a criminal record. Nothing serious. Petty childish stuff, but what makes matters worse is that his folks are good friends of mine. They're nice people and they're worried sick.'

'What do you want me to do?'

The policeman perched on the edge of the desk. 'I know you've involved young Jimmy in your boxing classes and given him plenty of encouragement so I wondered if you'd give him a character reference. It may help his case.' He hesitated. 'Perhaps you could have a word with Jimmy yourself?'

'No problem.' I assured him. 'Leave it to me.'

Despite being shocked by Jimmy's misdemeanours and pending court case, I nevertheless felt good at being asked to help in this way. I liked Jimmy. His ginger hair and spotty face reminded me of another Jimmy, my old pal from Aberdeen. So that evening I set about having a word with him, then sat down to write a character reference that might impress the court.

'Dear Sir,' I began with a flourish, then chewed my pen for the next five minutes waiting for an inspirational flow. Letter writing was not one of my strong points.

> Jimmy has been an active member of the boys' club for nearly a year now. He is a valuable member of the boxing team and has won several cups and trophies. He has a likeable and friendly manner and I have always found him to be fair and truthful.

I managed another two paragraphs extolling Jimmy's virtues and expressing the high hopes I had for him. I thought I might have overdone it a bit but nevertheless concluded:

> I am sure the punishment he received from his parents will have had an effect and the talk from our local bobby will certainly have struck home, but just to make sure, I have spoken firmly to Jimmy myself and warned him that if he doesn't damn well behave himself, I'll kick his arse from one end of the high street to the other.

> I trust this information will give you an adequate insight into Jimmy's character and his life at the boys' club.

> Yours faithfully,

> Alex Annand. Club Leader.

Fortunately for me, Jimmy appeared before a Judge in Chambers who had a great sense of humour. The policeman told me that if he had appeared in the Open Court, I could have found myself before the judge, charged with sending an abusive letter through Her Majesty's Postal Service.

Shortly after that Jimmy and his girlfriend attended the fortnightly club dance. I saw him and Jennie arrive. A bonnie little thing she was, with blue saucer eyes sparkling under a mop of bottle blonde hair and legs up to her chin. An hour later I was amused to see Jimmy's best friend, Bert, with his arms wrapped around her in the middle of the dance floor. I glanced around for Jimmy. There was no sign of him and as others were clamouring for my attention the matter was forgotten until nearer the end of the evening, when one of the smaller boys tore through the hall, his eyes almost popping out of his head.

'Fight out back, Alex! Quick! Jimmy's been in the working men's club next door drinking and he's come back drunk and found Bert with his girl! He's gonna kill him!'

I flew out to the back with one of the helpers hard on my heels and saw a terrified Bert pinned back against the railings by the rejected, drunken, red-headed boxer.

'JIMMY!' I bellowed. Racing over I dived between them just as Jimmy's right fist shot forward. There was a gasp from those around us as his grubby knuckles landed on my nose. Jimmy's facial expression changed to one of horror.

'Oh, Alex! I didn't mean to hit you!' He gulped and pointed in the direction of the amorous Romeo. 'It was him I was gonna kill! I wouldn't do anything to hurt you, not after what you done for me, writing to the courts and all that!'

As I dabbed my bloodied nose my fury swiftly abated. To be complimented in this way made me realise I had finally gained Jimmy's respect and trust and this I counted as a major breakthrough. Such was the manner in which my influence with the boys as well as my literary capabilities developed.

Although I'd exchanged addresses with my friends in the army I never heard from Ronnie again. He disappeared into his own little corner of the universe to make his mark. My friendship with Eric developed, though, as I discovered that he and his wife Lillian didn't live too far from me, and neither did his parents. They warmly welcomed me into their homes and fed me each time I poked my head through their door. In fact I began to spend as much time with them as I did with my own family.

Mick moved south. I wasn't to realise the full influence he'd had on my life until the boys' club was invited to a special service at the local church.

The vicar was a large, oval-faced, jovial young man aptly named Peter Jolly. He had a way of talking about Jesus which not only held my attention but strongly reminded me of Mick. As we left the church after that special service, I felt a strong desire to talk to him about this Jesus Christ whom he and Mick seemed to know so well. There were questions I wanted to ask to satisfy my curiosity but I was afraid it might appear that I was keen to get involved with Jesus and the church, and I wasn't. Well, not yet! I gave the customary handshake accompanied by a polite 'thank you' at the church door and was about to follow my lads out into the warm sunshine when I realised that the firm handshake hadn't let go.

'I believe you're the boys' club leader? Is that right?' he said, oblivious to the congestion he was causing in the doorway.

'Yes. That's right.'

'Thought so. My curate, Jonathan, is having problems with the church youth club. I wonder if there's any chance of you coming round to the vicarage to meet him sometime? I hear you've been pretty successful with the Broom Hill Club.'

I glowed with pride. 'Yes, I have,' I boasted unashamedly. 'I'd be delighted to come and talk to him. How about tomorrow?'

I discovered that Jonathan was not much older than myself. He was a slim, agile young man with hair that continually flopped in his eyes. I liked him immediately and somehow or other found myself attending the Sunday evening services then returning to his home for supper. Here was someone who would listen to my confused ramblings about religion and God without imposing his own views on me. The more we chatted, the more interested I became because Jonathan, like Mick, portrayed Jesus as a real person, someone akin to a close friend. Slowly, very slowly I was beginning to understand what that meant.

'But tell me something,' I said to him one Sunday as we made a few sandwiches and a pot of tea in his kitchen. 'How is someone like me supposed to meet this Jesus you're talking about? People have told me that God has spoken to them or answered their prayers, but how come he's never spoken to me or answered mine? That's a real hang-up with me, Jonathan.'

Jonathan spread a large dollop of tomato ketchup over the corned beef sandwich. 'Do you ever sit still long enough to listen, Alex? You're always on the go, always chattering. Perhaps he is trying to speak to you but he can't get a word in edgeways.'

We chatted easily over supper and late into the evening as we had done on many previous Sundays. Eventually I glanced at my watch. 'Time's getting on,' I said reluctantly. 'I'd better be away. I enjoy these stimulating conversations but they require a heck of a lot of brainwork.' I pulled on my overcoat and turned at the doorway. 'You can give me the answers to my questions next week after church, eh, Jonathan?'

'Answers?' He stood up slowly, a wry smile spreading across his face. 'No answers next week, Alex. You've got all the facts you need about Jesus. Now it's up to you.'

I frowned at him, puzzled. 'What d'you mean?'

'If you want this friend of mine, Jesus, in your life, all you have to do is ask. Go home and think about it.'

I walked home thinking about it. To be honest I'd done little else but think and talk to Jonathan about it over the past few weeks. It had been a constructive time for us both. I was helping him to run the church youth club and he in turn was helping me to discover new insights about God, Jesus Christ and the Christian Church. I had discovered that the army chaplain with his stiff regimental services was a far cry from the evangelical outlook of the Revd Peter Jolly and his curate Jonathan. They'd answered many of the questions of religion that had bothered me for so long and had impressed me by their faith and openness. Now, according to Jonathan, the ball was in my court.

It seemed ridiculous that I should spend a restless night tossing and turning and chewing over the conversations I'd had with Jonathan, but I did. I arrived at the Automobile Association the following day bleary-eyed and tired. The morning seemed eternal. My mind refused to concentrate on the pile of paperwork before me because I knew I was being faced with one of the biggest, if not the biggest, decision of my life. Jesus Christ seemed to infiltrate every pick-up truck and broken down limousine I read about, so that by the time my lunch hour arrived I was glad to get away.

Grabbing my sandwiches and flask I hurried off to meet a fairly new friend, Alan Witherington. Alan was warden of his local church, an intelligent, happy-go-lucky character, easy to talk to and a man of the world. He and I met regularly over lunch but my hunger that lunchtime went further than my stomach. I found myself in desperation pouring out my story to him and I didn't even get into a stew because they'd left the little blue bag of salt out of the packet of crisps. Alan listened patiently, munching a pork pie and nodding profoundly in all the right places.

'So what do you reckon?' I concluded.

The intellectual brow furrowed and I waited in anticipation for a profound statement that would clarify my confusion and make my decision for me.

'I dunno, Alex, I'm sure.'

'Don't know' wasn't quite what I had in mind.

'Perhaps,' he continued, 'You could go into St Nick's over there to pray about it?'

I glanced down the road where the tall spire of St Nicholas' Cathedral towered over the city centre. 'Think that'll help?'

'Dunno, Alex, but you could try it. I'll come with you if you like.'

We stepped inside the old gothic cathedral away from the roar of the traffic heading towards the bridge across the River Tyne and as the doors slammed behind us, a complete silence enveloped us. I stood with Alan behind me, uncertain what to do. There was a musty smell of old wood and beeswax polish. A few flowers had been decoratively arranged on a side table and window-sills, and a large golden cross and plate and cup stood on the altar. We made our way tentatively down to the front of the dark church, our footsteps echoing on the stone slabs. Occasionally a ray of sun streamed through the windows, sending a rainbow of colours across the walls. I heard Alan move into a wooden pew at the front and sit down but I continued forward to the altar and knelt down, wondering what to do.

'Father,' I whispered. My voice seemed to echo around the church. 'Father, I think I need to say, er . . . that I er . . . what I mean to say is, that if you want to come into my life, then I won't stop you.' Strange how once I'd started talking it seemed to get easier. 'I know I've made promises to you in the past and I've broken them, so if you're not really interested in me I'll understand, I really will, and I'm sorry now I didn't keep them but, er . . .' I hesitated. 'The fact of the matter is I want Jesus, you, to be part of my life. Like you are with Mick, Jonathan, Peter Jolly, Alan and er . . . I'd like it now, this minute! Please . . . Father. Amen.'

I heard a whispered 'Amen' behind me from Alan. There was no blinding flash or revelation, no voice of acceptance or rejection. Not even a tiny tongue of fire fell to show me that anything was any different. The church remained quiet and empty. Other than indigestion from onions I had eaten for lunch I wasn't aware of any change at all. Then later, at 3.30pm, while working at my desk, absorbed in a transcript of a car damaged by a herd of cows, I suddenly became aware of a growing sense of peace. All those doubts and fears and confused thoughts about religion and God seemed to be swept aside and I knew that at long last my time of turmoil was over. The sense of relief was enormous. I wanted to shout 'Hallelujah!', but I didn't think my boss would appreciate it so I stayed silent, nursing the growing knowledge inside me that Jesus Christ was now my Lord.

I glanced at my watch, willing the pointers round to 5 o'clock. There would be just enough time to call in and tell Jonathan what had happened before going home. At 5 o'clock I was first out of the office and first on the bus. At the appropriate stop I leapt off and ran down the street where Jonathan lived. He and the Revd Peter Jolly stood at the door. They turned and as they watched me running up the street towards them their faces broke out into wide smiles.

I flung open Jonathan's garden gate. 'I've found him!' I cried jubilantly.

Peter laughed, 'We know! The look on your face says it all, Alex! Welcome to the family of God, brother!'

↷ 12 ↶

The month that followed brought a number of unusually nice comments from people who knew me well. I was more contented, less rowdy and surprised everyone, including myself, by my lack of swearing. Even the lads at the boys' club started asking questions.

'What's up with you, Alex? You sick or in love or summat?'

'What do you mean?'

'You're . . . different.'

'How?'

'Just . . . different.'

I knew exactly what they meant but was unsure how to answer them. The opportunity presented itself one Saturday evening as I worked with a small group of boys tidying the church graveyard, a job the club had taken on as a community project. As usual it was late by the time we'd finished so, leaving them to put away the tools, I went to the local chip shop to buy a dozen portions of fish and chips and a few cans of Coke. When I returned dusk was falling, casting long eerie shadows from the tombstones over the wall of the church. It was a natural setting in which to provoke a lively discussion of life after death and tell the lads about my conversion experience.

A gentle breeze had sprung up, rustling the leaves of the trees and wafting the smell of fish and chips around the graveyard. As I talked about Jesus and my relationship with him, I felt strangely warm and alive. The boys sat transfixed and I wished with all my heart that they could find what I had been given.

Some weeks later I had the opportunity to further their discovery of Jesus when the Revd Peter Jolly asked me to organise a youth service in the church for Youth Sunday.

This special service was for all the young people in the area. It proved to be a huge responsibility, co-ordinating the various groups, organising a parade to the church, booking musicians, issuing invitations, working with the clergy to choose suitable hymns and ensuring that the whole service ran smoothly. Nothing of its kind had been seen in the area since before the war and it generated a great deal of interest in the community.

Peering through the main doors on the big day, I was thrilled to see the church packed to overflowing. Somewhere in that vast crowd was my family, apart from dad who declined the invitation to attend, since church had never been part of his life.

'Ready?' Peter and Jonathan, looking splendid in their robes, were to follow members of the armed forces in a small procession down the aisle. I nodded and a few minutes later the organ swelled to a crescendo as we moved into the body of the church to the singing of 'Onward Christian Soldiers'. When we reached the altar we took up our seats facing the congregation and I nervously scanned the crowded pews for my family. My eyes fell on Kathleen's red feather hat at the very front of the church. She gave me a saucy grin. Eileen, next to her, gave me a wink and my mam's and grandparents' faces shone with pride. There was a shuffling and scraping of chairs as the end of the procession took their seats, then the music faded away and silence fell upon the congregation.

Suddenly there was a clatter at the back of the church as a hymnbook was dropped and the door slammed. Curious heads turned. From my position facing the congregation I could see Emma, Peter's wife, shaking hands with someone, then indicating the rows of seats at the front. My pulse started to race, for walking down the aisle, for once without his cap, was the solitary figure of my father. He looked up as he reached the pews occupied by the rest of my family, caught my eye and gave me a nod of acknowledgement. The effort it must have cost him to come into church no one would ever know.

As the service got under way, I was filled with a sense of pride. My boys from the club had all turned up and sat squashed like sardines in the first few side pews. The youth club from church had all arrived and even all my family were supporting me in this special service that I had organised. Being together as a family in church was a brand new experience, something we'd never done before. It was the icing on the cake for me and as we sang the final hymn I breathed a prayer of gratitude: 'Thank you, God, for making this a perfect day!'

Over the months that followed my involvement with church and the people of the church grew. In fact I can't think of a time when I wasn't in church or with fellow Christians. New experiences followed new experiences and I was soon to discover that more were to come.

A few months after the special service I had an accident at a sports meeting for youth leaders. It was my own fault really. Encouraged by a few of the youth leaders to play half an hour of football, at which I was less than useless, I threw myself at the ball, missed and, with the full force of my body, slammed into the goalpost with an almighty crunch! Someone ran me to the hospital where I spent an uncomfortable couple of hours being prodded, X-rayed and finally diagnosed with a badly torn ligament in my shoulder. I was discharged with my arm in a sling and still in a great deal of pain.

On the way home I asked to be dropped off at the vicarage so I could beg leave of absence from the youth club the following evening. Emma answered the door and gasped when she saw my arm in a sling.

'Oh, Alex! What have you done to yourself? You poor thing. Come on in. I'll make you a nice cup of tea.'

Comforted by the warmth of her concern I decided that a cup of tea sounded like a good idea, especially if it was accompanied by more fuss and sympathy. She ushered me into their living room where Peter's concern equalled his wife's. They were entertaining a well-dressed, elderly couple who to my delight joined in the fuss by puffing up the cushions in the big comfortable armchair by the fire and carefully sitting me down.

'Thank you. Can you just push that cushion . . . thank you. Fine. Aahh!' I sank back. My arm was throbbing, my head was aching, my legs felt like jelly and I was still feeling slightly nauseous from shock . However, none of these things stopped me loving all the attention.

Emma bustled in with a fresh pot of tea. 'I hope you've introduced Dr McGregor and his wife to Alex, my love,' she said. 'Dr McGregor and his wife are retired missionaries, Alex.' She handed me a very black cup of tea.

Dr McGregor was a short, bald-headed man with the sort of open, smiling face that immediately made you feel you could trust him. His wife was a motherly, bird-like creature who twittered on, sugaring my tea and handing me biscuits.

'Oh? Where have you been working?' I asked, struggling to get my social graces into working order. To be truthful, now that the initial fussing was over and done with I couldn't have cared less where they'd been working. I was feeling so lousy I began to wish I'd gone straight home.

'Africa, mostly.' The missionary's faded blue eyes met mine, obviously aware of my discomfort.

'Dr McGregor was a leading surgeon in his field before he and his wife received the call to missionary work,' Peter said.

'Oh?' The sugary tea wasn't helping the waves of nausea.

'How did you have your accident?' Mrs McGregor chipped in.

'Some of us were playing football and I ended up arguing with the goalpost.'

'I don't like the way they've fixed that sling, Alex,' Emma frowned. 'I've seen a better job done on a baby's nappy!'

Peter winked. 'Once a nurse, always a nurse. Watch it, Alex. She's dying to sort it out.'

I smiled warily. I was grateful for the tea and concern, but not grateful enough to allow her to play nurse on me.

'What did the hospital say was wrong?' Dr McGregor placed a pair of bifocals on the end of his nose and sat forward in his seat, peering intently at my damaged arm. I shuffled uneasily. 'A torn ligament. Somewhere about . . . here.' I pointed vaguely to the area around my shoulder.

'Mmm.' The doctor cast a professional eye over my injury with interest.

'Mmm.' The nurse cast a professional eye over the sling.

I looked from one to the other apprehensively. 'Aye. Well, thanks for the tea.' I hastily gulped down the last dregs and made an ungainly attempt to get out of the chair filled with cushions.

'I'll just see to that sling before you go, Alex,' said Emma.

'Well, if you're taking the sling off, I'll just take a quick peek at that shoulder,' said the missionary.

'I'd better be on my way . . .'

Outnumbered and in too much pain to argue I sank back into the chair. Emma took off my sling and while she made a new one from an old linen sheet the doctor gently examined the offending injury, giving an occasional prod to convince himself he could still make his patients yelp. The slightest movement caused me a great deal of discomfort.

Eventually doctor and nurse sat back satisfied. I sat back exhausted.

'You should be more comfortable now Emma has fixed your sling, Alex, but perhaps we should have a word of prayer with you before you leave,' Peter said.

At least that couldn't be more painful than the agony they'd just put me through. However, much to my embarrassment, the four of them stood up and made a circle around my chair, placing their hands gently on my shoulder and head. I'd never experienced this type of praying before and wasn't too sure what was expected of me. I decided I couldn't go far wrong if I just sat still and quiet. Peter prayed first. He prayed for God's healing in such a quiet, gentle voice that I found myself relaxing back into the cushions. As Dr McGregor took up the praying I allowed all the tension and shock of the past few hours to drain out of me. I was very conscious of their love and concern.

I didn't really expect anything to happen. In my opinion I was feeling too ill for healing to take place, but that night I was surprised to find that, instead of struggling through a painful restless night, I slept deeply and comfortably. The nausea rapidly disappeared and by morning the pain had also gone. To my amazement, it never returned. I was puzzled over what had happened to me and began to replay their prayers over and over in my head, trying to make sense of it. Healing? I'd never thought of God as a healer before.

A few weeks later I called at the vicarage to discuss the youth club with Peter. As usual I was bursting at the seams with bright ideas and talked incessantly for the first twenty minutes before I became aware of him looking at me oddly. I raised my eyebrows questioningly, 'What's up?'

He didn't answer at first but sat ponderously tapping his desk with his forefinger. Then he took a long deep breath and said, 'Have you ever thought of offering your services for the ordained ministry, Alex?'

If ever I needed to be made speechless a question like that was bound to do it. My mouth dropped open in amazement. 'Eh?'

'I said, have you ever . . .'

'Yes, yes, I heard what you said but . . . the ministry? Are you mad?'

'No, I'm quite sane and quite serious. I think you would make a good minister.'

I shook my head. 'Haven't you got me mixed up with someone else?'

'No, and don't be so quick to condemn yourself or the idea.' He smiled at me.

'Think about it then we'll talk some more.'

I did think about it. In fact I thought of little else over the following weeks. I was flattered that someone I admired as much as Peter could even envisage me in such a profession as the ministry. The ministry! Yet it was strange how the idea seemed to develop the more I thought about it and before long I was convinced I was hearing it as a calling from God. I was seeing myself in a dog collar and enthusiastically making enquires as to how to set the ball rolling. I talked it through with mam over dinner one evening.

'I'm enrolling for O levels at evening school in September which will help me get into college, and next week I've an appointment with the archdeacon in Newcastle.'

'The ministry! The archdeacon! Och, Alex! It's a big step. Are you sure, son?' Dad looked up from his fireside chair where he was sitting reading the evening paper. He always hid behind it when I talked about the things of the church, but now he looked round it to say, 'You don't think you're getting a bit too religious do you, lad?'

I frowned at him. 'No!' I retorted sharply. 'I do not think I'm getting a bit too religious! I'm fed up with working at the AA and the ministry is something I want to do. Revd Jolly thinks I've a calling in that direction and that I stand a good chance of being accepted.'

'Aye. Maybe that's what he thinks, but you know you're not one for academic studies.'

'If I'm being called into the ministry, dad, God'll make sure I pass all my studies!' I told him confidently.

He snorted through his nose, leaving me in no doubt as to his opinion, and retired behind his paper again. Mam patted my arm reassuringly.

Dad was right of course. He generally was. I was no academic. I was always one to be doing rather than thinking, and having a full-time job, plus my voluntary work at the boys' clubs, kept me so busy there was little time left for the hard course of study I'd been warned about. Nevertheless I was so cocksure that I was such a bonus to the Christian Church that I was convinced Jesus would make sure I passed my exams. It therefore came as a devastating blow at the end of the course to be informed I'd failed. Numb with shock, I headed for Tynemouth beach to spend a solitary day walking along the sands, thinking.

Peter, Emma and Jonathan had been so sure that my call was to the ministry and had been so encouraging. What had gone wrong? The cold sea lapped over my toes, filling the imprints left by my feet. How could God have let me down like this? Perhaps I could have studied more, but surely if he really wanted me to be a minister in his church he could have given me a little bit of help?

'I gave you my life, Lord! Why didn't you want to use it? Don't you care what happens to me? Am I not worthy of serving you?' The lapping of the waves as they pounded up the beach and the cry of the seagulls hovering over Tynemouth priory were the only responses to my heartfelt cry. 'Where are you, God? Where are you?' I had never felt so angry, rejected and confused in my whole life.

Having believed that my days at the Automobile Association were numbered it was not only depressing to realise that I could be working there for the next forty years, but also humiliating trying to find answers for those folk curious about my sudden change of plans. The truth was, I had no answers. Not for others, and not for myself. God, it seemed, had abandoned me!

Fortunately I was never one to wallow in self-pity for long. I took a deep breath and threw myself back into my youth work till I'd had a chance to think about my next move.

One night I discussed some new ideas for the club with one of the helpers. 'A New Year's dance? That's a brilliant idea, Alex,' the helper enthused, as I outlined my plans.

'It will certainly be a way of bringing more members into the youth club,' I said, pleased by his response. 'I also thought a live band would be a good idea.'

'Yes, it would. I know of a group who would come. They're pretty reasonable, too.' I pondered for a moment. Although the church youth club had flourished and grown, the membership was still predominantly female. There was table tennis and a few other things of interest, but a dance would serve to encourage the lads to join us.

For the next hour or so we sat discussing the plans I'd jotted down on the back of a tatty old envelope. This was just the sort of challenge I needed to take my mind off the last disastrous few weeks.

'All you have to do now, Alex, is have a word with Peter Jolly and Jonathan to get their approval, then we're flying.'

I did have a word!

'No! Absolutely not, Alex!'

Jonathan shuffled uncomfortably in his seat as I looked from Peter to him in amazement.

'But why not?' I asked in astonishment. 'It would bring in much-needed money for the youngsters and the church and it would also encourage youngsters to join the club!'

Peter shook his head firmly. 'It would also be a tool for Satan.'

'Eh? A tool for Satan? How?'

'It'll not be the Church of Jesus that attracts the young lads in, but our young ladies.' 'Nothing wrong with that. It's a natural part of growing up.'

'Is it? The sort of evening you're suggesting is giving an opportunity for close physical contact and the Lord only knows where that might lead!'

'Where that might . . !' I raised my voice in disbelief. 'Peter, we're talking about young kids, decent kids, with a good understanding of right and wrong.'

'Yes, and it's our job to keep it that way. The whole idea of the youth club is to share Jesus with them.'

'I agree. But it's also our job to help these kids grow up and face the temptations in life.'

'Yes, face them, not put them in their path. The answer is still no,' Peter said firmly. I stared at him aghast, struggling to understand this strange line of reasoning. I'd already spent a great deal of time and effort in planning this venture and received overwhelming support from the youth club members. I glanced over at Jonathan, hoping for moral support but he averted his eyes. He was, after all, Peter's curate.

'Peter's right,' he mumbled. 'It's inviting temptation and we're not in the business of doing that, Alex.'

I looked from one to the other, exasperated. 'Temptation!' I exploded. It had been a long time since I'd lost my temper. 'Temptation! I'm not talking about opening a bloody brothel! I'm talking about a church youth club dance on church premises with responsible leaders present to celebrate New Year!'

'I've given you my answer, Alex.' Peter's usual round jovial face wore the fixed expression of one determined he would not be moved on this issue.

'You could have a party with games,' suggested Jonathan. 'Proper games like pass the parcel, a quiz, musical chairs. Not one that encourages close bodily contact between young people.'

His remarks left me stunned.

'I've never heard such bloody rubbish in all my life!' I exploded.

We talked. Or rather they talked and I shouted around the subject a while longer. Eventually Jonathan suggested we leave.

'Where does it say in the Bible that men and women shouldn't have close contact?' I stormed as we walked home.

'Well, it . . .'

'The Christian gospel is about love. How can you experience love if you don't have fellowship?'

'You're distorting the point, Alex. We believe . . .'

'We believe, Jonathan? We? Don't tell me you agree with him?'

Jonathan looked uncomfortable. 'I think I do, Alex.'

'Think! You only think you do?'

'I don't want to discuss it. I'm under Peter's authority and he's doing a grand job bringing people into the church without having to have dances and the like.'

We walked home in an angry silence and our farewell was far from friendly. I took the long way home. I needed time to think – again! I couldn't believe the two people I admired most could be so narrow-minded and bigoted. True, both Peter and Jonathan were a refreshing change from the stiff army chaplain wrapped up in his high ideals of duty, service and rituals, but now I wasn't so sure that Peter and Jonathan weren't just as wrapped up in their own ideals as he was.

I joined in the usual Christmas festivities, going to nightclubs, parties and dances with my friends, but I was uncomfortable knowing that in the eyes of Peter and Jonathan I could be inviting Satan to do his work. I really couldn't believe that what I was doing was an open invitation to sin and sex, and came to the conclusion that if they were so blinkered and that this was their brand of Christianity, I didn't like it!

I started the New Year in a bitter frame of mind. That my Christian faith was being somewhat shaken was an understatement. I was at a loss to know how to deal with the reactions of the two people who'd had such an influence on my life! It was almost as though the devil had decided to sow seeds of doubt in my mind about my relationship with Jesus and his people, and my call into the ministry. Firstly I'd failed my exams which cancelled out the ministry for me. Then I'd been refused permission to organise a church dance which made me feel rejected by the church. But the final blow came when Peter found me locking up after the youth club one evening. 'We're moving, Alex. It's just been confirmed. I've been offered a job down south and Jonathan is going to join me. You're one of the first people we've told.' He looked at me, willing me to understand, pleading for me to return to the warm friendship we'd shared. I shook my head in despair. How could they do this to me?

Who was this God who could lead me up the garden path towards the Christian Church and then slam the door in my face? And now, in the midst of my confusion, could remove the two people I relied on most? I did indeed feel as if they and God were abandoning me, and for many weeks almost tore myself apart wondering if this was some sort of punishment. It wasn't a sudden decision, but one that was reached slowly in my mind over a period of time. It just so happened that in the week that the Revd Peter Jolly, Emma and Jonathan moved to their new appointments, I severed my contacts with the church and its youth club and then turned my back on God.

If they could reject me and hurt me like this then I had no need of any of them! I could manage very well on my own, thank you very much!

∞ 13 ∞

I broke into a trot across the courtyard as a heavy cloud overhead threatened to break before I reached the school entrance.

'Alex!' A call from the headmaster attracted my attention. 'I'd like a word with you this evening about the camping trip if you can spare the time.'

'Right!' I waved in acknowledgement then bounced up the steps and into the hallway where the clatter of dishes and smell of burnt custard warned me that the evening meal was in progress. Somewhere in the background a television droned and upstairs an argument between two of the boys had broken out. I ignored it. Someone else would have to deal with them. I had enough on my hands organising the camping trip. Whistling happily I took the stairs to my room two at a time, locking myself in so I could plan last minute details.

The headmaster of the approved school where I now worked saw this camping trip as a new venture for the school and I was keen to support him. Many of the kids were there because of their criminal activities but basically they were just children and, as experience had already taught me, they responded well to new challenges.

It seemed a lifetime away but it was only a year since I had failed my O levels and had the doors of the ministry closed in my face. The departure of Peter and Jonathan had left me unsettled and aimless for some months. However, never being one to wallow in the doldrums for long, I had shaken off all that religious nonsense and set about getting down to what I called 'real living'. The opportunity came when I heard through the grapevine of a job working with children with problems and difficulties and I decided to apply for the post.

'You'll never get a job like that, Alex.' George shook his head in disbelief that I'd even had the nerve to apply.

'You're not qualified enough,' Eric said when I told him the news. 'You're aiming for the moon again.'

I don't know who was the most amazed, them or me, when I landed the post of housemaster at the approved school and joined the staff. I enjoyed my new job, apart from the task of taking the boys to the local church each Sunday morning. Week after week seventy-two boys and their housemasters sat through a dry, lifeless service and it seemed to me that the only time the vicar paid us any attention was when one of the boys misbehaved. Otherwise we were virtually ignored. With angry satisfaction I realised it bore out my theory that the Church did not have time for the likes of these lads, or me! Past experiences had left me very hurt and bitter.

My previous experience of working with youth clubs was useful and gave me a distinct advantage but I soon had to learn how to become a firm disciplinarian, for these were boys with anti-social and behavioural problems, many of whom had committed crimes and all of whom were here by order of the courts. I soon discovered that my army training had not been wasted and barked out orders like a sergeant-major. This was especially beneficial when dealing with boys who were as high as kites with excitement over their forthcoming camping trip.

The following morning brought clear blue skies and warm sunshine. Just what we needed for a week in a tent. Two other members of staff and I packed camping equipment into the back of the minibus, counted the boys into the vehicles then drove to a site near Amble, a fishing port on the Northumberland coast. Hardly any of the lads had been camping before and despite mock camping exercises in the school grounds it still took them the best part of the afternoon to erect something resembling a tent that would offer reasonable shelter from the inevitable north-east wind and rain. Eventually, after some sort of order had been restored, I decided to take a leisurely stroll along the beach towards the harbour, returning to the camp site via the road to see if there was a shop in the village where I could order a daily supply of groceries.

There was, and it was the strangest of places. It was a house which appeared to double up as a shop. The living room had tables and work surfaces strewn with sweets, pickles, bread and general necessities and the shelves along the walls were packed with tins. But what drew my attention almost immediately were the gentle, grey-blue eyes that met and held mine.

'Can I help you?' she asked.

My mind went a complete blank. 'Er . . . yes . . . er . . . I . . .' She was tall, five feet six inches or so, only two or three inches shorter than me, and a pale blue dress hugged her slender figure. My stare must have unnerved her because she turned a gentle shade of pink.

'A tin of black bullets, please,' I stammered.

She came from behind the counter and stood on the stool beside me to reach a tin of the sweets from one of the top shelves. 'Is that all?' She turned and saw me giving her the once-over and the pink turned into a deeper shade of red.

'Groceries!' I said, suddenly remembering the reason for my visit. 'I'm camping at the site down the road with lads from our school. Can you supply milk and bread for us?'

'I'll . . . I'd better get my mam!' She jumped down from the stool and fled through a door at the back of the room. A moment later the stocky figure of her mother appeared.

'Now then,' she said in a deep Northumbrian accent, 'How can I help you?'

I repeated my request for groceries, hoping the girl would come back into the room, but she didn't and I was left with the mental image of those gentle, grey-blue eyes and slim figure which stayed with me all the way back to camp.

Suddenly the holiday had taken on a new dimension. Every morning I found myself up and shaved at the crack of dawn and accompanying a couple of the boys to the shop for the groceries. I soon found that there were no regular shop hours. If you wanted something you simply knocked on the door. In fact it wasn't unknown for the local miners on night-shift to knock them up at 2.00am. 'Elsie! Can I have a packet of Woodbines?'

I discovered that the girl's name was Eva and she helped her mother run the shop, but despite all my efforts to draw her into conversation she remained quiet and reserved and I came to the conclusion that she was either extremely shy or she didn't like Scotsmen.

One hot but very windy afternoon, just before the end of the holiday, the other two housemasters took the boys to the beach to give them free reign. I set off for a leisurely stroll along by the harbour, hoping for an hour or so by myself to watch the sea pounding up to the harbour wall. One or two fishing boats came in, seeking shelter from the high winds. Screeching seagulls hovered overhead, hoping for scraps. Despite the high wind it was a very pleasant afternoon and I thoroughly enjoyed myself. I was wearing my kilt. I wore it rarely these days, but being only a few miles south of the Scottish border it wasn't an uncommon sight.

I decided to meander back to the campsite via the shop. Not that I wanted anything but there was always the chance I would bump into Eva. I hovered around the half-open door for a moment, trying to think of something other than black bullets to purchase. Amazingly we were always running short of something at camp even though we'd come well-prepared and of course it was always me that discovered the shortage and had to walk to the shop. Even when we were overstocked I still found an excuse for a visit. I was rapidly acquiring an accumulation of black bullets and other bits and pieces for which we had no use and, frustratingly, the visits weren't bringing me any closer to inviting her out. Other than being polite when serving me or giving me an embarrassed wave when I saw her walking across the cliffs with her friend, there'd been no encouragement at all from her.

Suddenly the familiar strains of a popular Scottish song filtered through the upstairs window:

> Let the wind blow high, let the wind blow low,
> Through the streets in my kilt I'll go,
> All the lassies say 'Hello,
> Donald, where's yer troosers?'

Surprised and faintly amused I glanced up towards the open bedroom window and caught her peering around the curtains at me. As she darted out of sight I contained a chuckle of amusement. Straightening my shoulders and coming to attention, I pursed my lips and began whistling the second verse of the song. Then I broke into a military march down the High Street, my kilt swinging to and fro in the wind. Play games with me, would she? I'd teach her.

Unfortunately I didn't have time to teach her anything as our camping holiday was over before I had time to think up my next move. I did try calling at the shop the following evening, hoping to catch a glimpse of her. But her mother was serving a customer and her father was busy at the back clearing out the ashes and she was nowhere to be seen. Disappointed, I left the shop and the following day we packed up our tents and belongings and left Amble.

I told Eric and his wife Lillian about her on one of my frequent visits to their home for a meal.

'You should have asked her out, Alex,' Lillian remonstrated.

'I dinna think she's really interested. Anyway, the holiday was nearly over.' I peered into the big brown earthenware dish. 'Is there any more of that pudding, Lillian?'

'Help yourself.' She watched amused as I piled my pudding dish high. 'Heaven help the poor lass who has to feed you, Alex Annand,' she said shaking her head. 'Eric, pass the custard to Alex.'

I grunted. My mouth was full of pudding.

'What makes you think she's not interested?' Eric asked, looking inside the jug of custard. He poured a small amount over my pudding, obviously decided I'd had enough and poured the rest into his own bowl.

I shrugged. 'She didn't show it.'

'Did it ever occur to you the poor lass was shy?'

It had, but I was convinced that she would have responded in some way to my open, friendly manner. Most folks did.

'I think you should have a run back there and ask her out,' Eric said.

'Reckon?' I asked.

'Aye, but I'd not tell her how much you eat. We don't want to put her off straight away!' Lillian remarked dryly.

A couple of days later I walked into the shop with knocking knees. Fortunately I wasn't wearing my kilt. Not a flicker of emotion showed in her eyes as I asked her out, although she did turn a gentle shade of pink and lowered her eyelashes. Somehow I was aware of a great sense of humour lurking beneath the quiet exterior and I was anxious to discover more.

A trip to the pictures was a rare occurrence for Eva. Her lifestyle had been so sheltered that even a day spent in Newcastle city centre, just over thirty miles away, was an adventure for her.

When you fall in love, you fall in love and there's nothing you can do about it except marry the girl. When that decision had been made everything else seemed to fall into place, even to the headmaster offering us one of the new houses being built in the grounds of the school. Eva happily and calmly set about organising our wedding in Amble and buying curtains and furniture for our new home

117

while I excitedly and noisily raced around being more of a hindrance than a help.

On the day before our wedding, our relatives began crawling out of the woodwork. Well, mine did. They arrived off trains, buses and in cars of all makes and descriptions, and by the time I returned to my parents' house from school, the celebrations were well under way for my stag night.

I think I enjoyed it. Well, they tell me I did. My only recollections were of falling over unidentifiable bodies in the dark as we returned to the house. I fumbled my way up the stairs and into my old bedroom which I was sharing with yet another cousin. Leaving my suit and underclothes where I stepped out of them, I rolled into bed with a vague awareness that the hump next to me had taken more of his fair share of the mattress. Too tired to care, I fell into an exhausted sleep on the edge of the bed.

The strains of birds singing and someone snoring brought me consciously into the world on my wedding day. Drowsily I opened one bleary eye. I was relieved to see the sun shining through the curtains. Having to travel thirty miles or so to Amble in early March, the weather had been our main concern. I stretched, relieving the parts that had had a hard night hanging out of the bed, and the snores changed into a splutter. Slowly I opened both eyes. A pair of pink and white dentures grinned back at me from a glass of water on the bedside table. Strange. Cousin Jack didn't have false teeth, did he? A horrible suspicion filtered through to my sleepy brain. Cautiously I rolled over and the figure beside me stiffened. Sharply turning my head I came face to face with a pair of shocked, faded, pale blue eyes, wrinkled skin, pink gums and a hairnet.

'Granny!' I yelped. I leapt out of bed, grabbing the pillow to provide some form of modesty. 'What are you doing here?'

The pink gums grinned at me. 'I've come to your wedding, Alex,' Granny chuckled. 'Och! It's been fun so far and it hasna even started yet!'

It was a bright, clear and crisp March morning as the family convoy set off for Amble, but by the time we'd covered ten miles, snow clouds had descended and the first flakes were leaving a fine covering on the roads.

'Divna worry, Alex. We'll get there. There'll no' be a problem on your wedding day.'

I didn't realise that the problem lay not with the groom and his best man but with the bride-to-be and her bridesmaids, who'd been taken to the hairdresser's early that morning.

Their return journey had been hampered by the car breaking down followed by a heavy fall of snow, and as I glided up the A1 to Amble, my future bride and her bridesmaids were pushing their car back to the house while the snow left its tiny wet flakes over their expensively styled hairdos.

My stag night may have slipped into oblivion but my wedding day was one to be remembered. Being a social animal I thrived on the attention and compliments and laughed, joked and chattered incessantly to every one of our two hundred and thirty guests.

'Mr Annand, if you and your wife would like to stand here . . .' the photographer hovered around us, moving us this way and that after the service.

'Uncle Alex!' I bellowed. 'Hey! We haven't had a picture with you and Auntie Audrey yet . . .'

'Mr Annand. If you could just move to your left . . .' Eva gently manoeuvred me into position.

'Hey, Eric! Lillian! We'll have you on the next one.' I stepped forward as I shouted. The photographer took my sleeve and pushed me back into place. 'Mr Annand. Would you please stand still for one . . .'

I ignored him. 'Geoff! Great to see you!'

'Mr Annand! Please!'

'Anyone want a photo with . . !'

'Mr Annand! If you could just shut your mouth long enough to smile, we might get these blasted photos taken!'

Eva quietly giggled at my side.

My speech was brilliant!

' . . . and finally,' I concluded in my big booming voice, 'I have a confession to make to all you good folks . . . and my new wife.'

Eva looked up at me curiously.

'We begin a new era, Eva and me,' I continued, 'and I want to start it with a clean slate.' I could sense the curiosity around the room and allowed the pause to linger. My father gave me a warning frown and my mother clasped her hands nervously in her seat. I lowered my voice. 'I'd like you to join me as I propose a toast to a very special lady.' All eyes turned towards Eva and she shuffled, uncomfortable at being in the limelight. 'Raise your glasses, please, to . . . to the lady I slept with last night!' There was a deathly hush around the room and one or two embarrassed laughs as I lifted my glass.

'Ladies and gentlemen. I give you – my Granny!'

Married life with poor Eva had begun.

‹ﾟ 14 ﾟ›

It was a two-bedroomed flat, certainly not as big as the house we had left at the approved school but enough for the three, soon-to-be-four of us. I turned to Eva. 'Do you like it?'

'Mmm.' I could see that in her mind's eye she was hanging curtains, laying carpets and arranging furniture. 'I think it'll be nice and I've always loved Alnmouth.'

I relieved her of our year old plump, rosy-cheeked daughter smelling of milk and talcum powder, and we stood in silence looking out of the window. This quiet, historical seaside village on the Northumbrian coast attracted tourists in the summer and historians all year round. Other than a few shops, its main street leading to the sea consisted of old hotels with slated roofs, oak beams and their fair share of ghosts. A few bed and breakfast houses and a golf course overlooked the sea and sand dunes.

'What's that place across the road, Alex?' Eva pointed to a large, rambling stone building on the hill, half-hidden by trees and bushes in its spacious grounds.

'It's the friary.'

'It's beautiful.' Abruptly she changed the subject. 'As we'll be seeing a bit more of you from now on, the decorating shouldn't take too long, should it?'

The gentle dig did not go unnoticed, and I felt a pang of guilt. It hadn't been an easy start for Eva. She had been left to decorate and set up our first home single-handed while I, encouraged by the headmaster, had gone off to spend a year at training college in Birmingham to obtain my qualifications. I returned at weekends, whenever I could afford it, to be with my new bride.

On my return from college extra duties and responsibilities for housemasters had resulted in longer hours which meant

I still hardly saw her or my new daughter, Rae. It was when talks suggesting further changes in working hours began that I decided it was time for me to move on.

'Do you think we could afford new curtains, Alex?'

'Probably not, but no doubt I'll arrive home one evening to find them hanging up.' She chuckled. 'With the little extra money you're making we could probably stretch to them. We deserve something nice.'

'So I'm treating myself to a new pair of living room curtains?' I remarked dryly. 'Just what I always wanted.'

My interview for this post of full-time youth worker for a boys' club and training centre had gone well and I'd been offered the job. Unfortunately there'd been a last minute hitch. The Department of Education and Science refused to recognise my housemaster qualifications. Bitterly disappointed and somewhat angry, I silently scorned Eva's comments that 'Somebody up there is looking after you and it's all in his hands.' But a few weeks later I received a letter from the Chairman of the Boys' Club Movement, who also happened to be a peer of the realm. Disagreeing with the Department's response, he had written to them arguing that in view of the shortage of qualified youth leaders and the fact that much of my course in Birmingham had included lectures and training in youth club work, my application should be reconsidered. After a few anxious weeks a letter arrived confirming that I had been given special recognition as a qualified youth leader, and so Eva, Rae and our new born baby son, Iain, and I moved to Alnmouth so that I could take up my new post.

I found it incredible that my case had been discussed at such a high level. After all, it was hardly a high-ranking post. I also found it hard to dismiss Eva's comment that 'Somebody up there is looking after you' because, strange as it seemed, I once again found myself thrust back into the company of Christians. This time it was the friars of Alnmouth.

I discovered this holy order of Franciscan Brothers to be a dedicated body of men in prayer, teaching, hospitality, evangelism and service and since the Father Guardian of Alnmouth Friary, Father Michael, was also chairman of the Youth Committee, frequent visits to the priory were inevitable. I never met such an easygoing man as Father Michael. He had a wonderful way of listening and making you feel that what you had to say was important. Consequently I found myself discussing not only the issues of the Youth Club but minor worries that the move to Alnmouth had brought. 'Why don't you and your family join us for our Christmas concert, Alex?' His kindly face was transformed by a beaming smile as the idea came to him. 'It'll help you get to know us and the folks hereabouts.'

I hesitated, flattered that he'd asked me yet apprehensive at the thought of getting involved with Christians again.

'Well, er . . . what with the new baby and, er . . . sleepless nights . . .'

He nodded understandingly but I had the distinct impression he could read far more into my excuses than I wanted him to. As it happens they were justifiable excuses as young Iain cried every night so Eva declined Father Michael's kind invitation and, begging exhaustion, left me to attend by myself.

I slammed the front door shut behind me and stepped into the cold night air followed by screams of 'Dadad' from Rae and howls from Iain. A blustery north-east wind from the sea tore through the trees and bushes, casting uneven shadows across my path as I hurried up to the friary entrance. As I stepped inside the large square, dimly-lit hall with its marble arches and dark corners, the door slammed behind me, leaving me in an eerie silence. For a moment I wondered if I'd confused the evening of the concert, then I heard a wailing, a bit like a cat being strangled, from the top of the stairs.

'Hello? Anybody there?' My footsteps echoed across the old, highly-polished wooden floor as I made my way cautiously towards the wide marble staircase. I hesitated halfway up the spacious landing with its enormous bay window overlooking the sea. By now the cat was sounding a little less strangled and a bit more like a fiddle. At the top of the stairs stood a thick oak door. I opened it. The brightly lit room, with a roaring log fire at one end and a partially set table at the other was warm and inviting. Books and pictures filled the walls and chairs and cushions were scattered around the floor of this enormous library. On one of the chairs was seated a demure little man in his mid-sixties extracting weird noises from his fiddle. He looked up expectantly when I poked my head curiously around the door.

'Hello. You must be the new youth club leader. I'm Father Jo.' The wide smile that broke across his face sent wrinkles to his ears.

'Aye. I popped across at Father Michael's invitation and heard you er . . . rendition in the corridor. I play the mandolin myself.'

'Really?' He wore that half-expectant expression that didn't need to ask if we shoud try a duet.

'Shall I go and get it? We'll have a set-to with the old strings?'

'Oh my. Oh yes. A set-to with the old strings.' He suddenly frowned. 'The only thing is I'm supposed to be helping in the kitchen.' He grinned at me. 'Well, I won't let on if you don't.'

I laughed. 'Right!' There was certainly nothing wrong with this chap. 'Back in two minutes.'

Eva looked up in surprise as I rushed back into the flat. 'Hello, you're back early. That's nice.' she teased.

'Er . . . yes, love.' I gave her a quick peck on the cheek as I grabbed my mandolin then slammed the door shut on my way out again.

Father Jo turned out to be a genius on the fiddle and was in his element having a fellow musician join him. One by one the friars and a mixed bag of guests, including a few locals and homeless people staying for Christmas, wandered into the library carrying huge plates of food and I soon found it increasingly difficult to contain my mirth as these holy men of God threw themselves wholeheartedly into jigging around in time to the music in their old faded trousers, darned jumpers and open-toed sandals.

Time disappeared in a comfortable evening of music, mimes, stories, poetry and laughter around the roaring log fire so that by the time nine o'clock came I felt I'd known these chaps for years. I glanced at my watch guiltily. I'd better be away home. Eva would be wondering where I was. There were moans of disappointment but they didn't try to persuade me to stay. However, they wouldn't let me leave without a plate of mince pies for Eva, a jug of milk and presents for the children. Regretfully I left the friary amidst a chorus of 'Merry Christmas, Alex!' mixed in with a great deal of hilarity. I couldn't believe I'd had such a good night. Not amongst Christians anyway!

As I quietly closed the big double door of the friary behind me, the biting north-east wind from the sea cut through my jacket like a knife. Wrapping my scarf around my face and breathing into it to create a bit of warmth for my nose, I wound my way along dimly lit path of the friary. Trees and bushes either side of me waved wildly in the wind, making the path difficult to see. I didn't want to trip, not with my arms full of goodies. I was concentrating so hard I almost missed the 'Merry Christmas, Alex!' from two young novices in civilian clothes turning into the gates of the friary.

'Here, we'll give you a hand with this lot,' one of them said.

126

'Thanks, lads.' We distributed the mandolin case, milk, mince pies and presents between us. 'Been out celebrating?'

They laughed cautiously. 'Er, you could say that.' A whiff of alcohol wafted in my direction. 'We should have been in before now but . . .'

' . . . but we were sidetracked.' They laughed guiltily like two conspirators.

'Have a good Christmas, Alex,' they called as they left me on the doorstep of my home. I entered the house chuckling. No doubt they would be severely reprimanded for coming in late and glassy-eyed, but tonight had certainly dispelled any earlier apprehensions I might have had at having to deal with such a solemn holy order. Here were men of God able to enjoy themselves alongside their Christianity, and for the first time since I'd left the church the name 'Christian' didn't leave a sour taste in my mouth.

The Brothers from the friary were always popping over to see us at the youth club, not least because of the two superb snooker tables. Surprisingly, a number of them were quite good players.

I was cleaning the brightly-lit bar where we served coffee when Brother Aiden walked in one morning. His hairy knee protruded through torn jeans and a brown darn sat visibly at each elbow of his green baggy sweater. 'How's the little 'un, Alex?' he asked, scratching his beard.

I looked up, bleary-eyed. 'Don't ask! He squawked all night and woke up Rae. Eva ended up pacing the bedroom floor with him while I made drinks and read stories to my daughter to get her back to sleep. What a night!'

Brother Aiden laughed. He was one of the most unthreatening Christians I'd ever come across. This gentle Franciscan with his lively sense of humour was the sort of bloke I could relate to and not surprisingly we had become good friends. He perched on the stool by the coffee bar. 'Fancy a game of snooker, Alex?'

I threw the tea towel in the corner. 'Aye, why not? I could do with a bit of light relief. It's been one o' them there days, and nights!'

Brother Aiden picked up a cue. 'It must be hard on little Iain coming into the big wide world and not being able to tell you what he wants.'

'I know what he wants all right!' I tossed a coin. It landed heads up so I broke the reds. 'Food. That's all that lad wants. Damn!' I surveyed the table in disgust as the cue ball disappeared down a pocket. I could see this wasn't going to be one of my better games.

Brother Aiden potted the next half-dozen balls without effort. 'If I win you can make the tea Alex, OK?'

I grunted non-committally as I aimed at what should have been an easy red. I gave it my best shot – and missed.

'You've not got the magic touch today, Alex,' Brother Aiden taunted as he took up his position. I stared in disbelief as he knocked ball after ball into the pockets.

'You jammy . . !' I caught the swear-word just in time. Brother Aiden may have been a friend, but he was after all a man of the cloth, albeit in raggy jeans and a darned sweater. He straightened up. 'I think "jammy bugger" is the phrase you're looking for, Alex.' Slightly shaken by his language I looked up. 'I didn't know you could say that!'

He raised his eyebrows and there was a moment's hesitation before he said, 'The difference between you saying it and me is that when I swear I have to do a penance for it.'

'Oh.' I deliberately didn't continue the conversation as I had no desire to give him the opportunity to embark on a theological discussion. I'd been down that path with Peter and Jonathan and look where it had got me! I might still respect them as individuals who were doing a good job but their extreme views had left me distraught and confused. I potted a ball and moved around the table.

'Good shot!' Brother Aiden obviously had his mind on snooker, not theology. That was what I liked about these gentle Franciscan Brothers. They were so very different from the army chaplain and from Peter and Jonathan. Never once had any of them tried to force their beliefs down my throat or try to prove that theirs was the 'right way'. Working in close proximity with these men I was able to observe a religious order that was not only simple and hardworking but had an attitude to life that I could respect and, more importantly, understand. Gradually I was beginning to have a more balanced view of God and these good Christian people, and for some strange reason that remark over the snooker table from Brother Aiden seemed to confirm my new ideas.

However, I wasn't given much more time to see the Franciscans' brand of Christianity in action as not long afterwards Father Michael called me into the office and almost apologetically told me he was leaving.

'I shall miss you, Alex, and our little chats but I feels it's God's calling for me to move on to another friary.'

'But . . . but the boy's club is just starting to pick up and I had plans I wanted to discuss . . .' I trailed off, realising how pathetic I sounded. The truth was I had become quite attached to this gentle friar who had patiently listened to all my bitter ramblings over Peter and Jonathan yet had never condemned either them or me for our disagreement. It was a sad day for the friars and for me when he left and an even worse day when the new Chairman of the Management Committee arrived. He was a hard-headed businessman in a smart suit and conservative tie and I was called into his office for a discussion about my future almost before I'd had a chance to get used to Father Michael's departure. It wasn't a pleasant interview.

'I'm afraid you'll have to go. There aren't enough kids in the club and frankly, Mr Annand, the grant for your salary has been withdrawn so we can no longer afford to keep you.' There wasn't a hint of an apology in his tone.

'But . . . but . . . I've said repeatedly we'd have to pick up on club membership.' I struggled to keep control of the rising anger inside me. 'When Father Michael . . .' 'Father Michael has moved on.'

'More's the pity!' I snapped. I could have bitten my tongue off. The last thing I needed to do was lose my temper. 'Look. Couldn't I ask you to reconsider? I have a wife and two small children to provide for.'

'I'm sorry, Mr Annand. All I can do is give you one month's notice. Hopefully you will be able to find other accommodation and employment by then.'

I stood for a moment wondering if it was worth an argument but decided against it. His mind was obviously firmly made up.

I left the office hurt and angry, more with myself than anybody else. I'd been somewhat outspoken some weeks ago, stating what I believed we should do in the way of running the club. Unfortunately I'd upset the wrong person and I was sure that he had pulled strings within the system to get rid of me, although I could never prove it. Now for the first time in my life I didn't know where to go or what to do.

Telling Eva was worse. A worried frown furrowed across her brow. 'So what'll we do, Alex? Where'll we live?'

I sat in the armchair while Rae clambered all over me. 'I don't know, Eva, I'm sure, but don't worry, love, I'll think of something.'

Trouble was, I couldn't think of a thing. There were no jobs in the small village of Alnmouth and even if there were, I had to find accommodation. As the end of the month drew closer and the time came to leave the flat our sense of panic increased.

'Still nothing?' Eva wiped her hands on the tea towel and turned to greet me as I came through the door.

I hesitated. 'No jobs, love, no, but I've been making enquiries about the cost of storing furniture.'

'Storing furniture?' She stood twisting the tea towel nervously in her hands. 'And how are we supposed to live without furniture, Alex?'

'We'll not have a roof over our heads in a week, never mind damned furniture!' I snapped and instantly regretted my outburst as her eyes filled up with tears. Wordlessly she returned to the kitchen. Our nerves were taut with the strain of the past month.

I sighed and followed her. 'Oh, Eva. I'm sorry.' I wrapped my arms around her, feeling her shaking as pent-up tears fell on my shirt. Eventually she calmed down and still nestling in my shoulder murmured, 'What are you going to do, Alex?'

I hugged her. 'If I canna get a job in a couple o' days we've only one alternative.' She waited for me to continue. 'We'll put the furniture into storage and you can move in with your mam.'

She looked up at me, frowning. 'But, Alex, there's no room for all of us.' Realisation dawned. 'And you, Alex? Where'll you be?'

I couldn't look at her when I said, 'I'm bound to get work in the city, Eva. I'll stay with my mam and dad in Newcastle till I do.' We stood silently in the kitchen with our arms around each other. No words could convey our desperate fears for the future.

At the end of the week Eva and the children and their suitcases moved to Amble to live for an indefinite period with her parents. Later that day, I helped to pack the last of our furniture into the removal van and watched helplessly as our belongings were driven away. I wandered back into the silent, empty flat, fighting off the waves of disappointment that everything had turned out this way. Thrusting my hands into my pockets I looked out of the windows towards the friary.

131

'Oh, Father Michael,' I whispered. 'if only you were here.'

Autumn leaves of yellow, brown and red had fallen around the friary making a colourful carpet. Rae had played happily among them yesterday, laughing delightedly as they crunched beneath her feet, while above her in the trees, the hardiest of leaves clung on, waiting for the day when they too would surrender to the winter weather. 'At least when you've fallen you can't sink any lower,' I reflected. I was wrong. I hadn't experienced being trampled underfoot.

Our parents were kind and supportive but a few days later when I visited Eva and the children at her mother's home, we were both upset when I had to leave and I suffered acute pangs of guilt that I had not been able to provide a home for them. It was not a happy visit and I was actually glad to return to my parents' home in Newcastle. A few weeks later I landed a job as a taxi driver.

'It's a poor wage but it's only a stop-gap,' I informed Eva during one of my visits. 'Just till something better turns up.

Working nine or more hours a day, from early evening to three or four the following morning brought me into contact with the seedier side of life. I felt desperately lonely, and fed up with the anti-social hours I worked. Soon I was deeply depressed. I was always tired, longed to see daylight and couldn't see any hope for the future. For months my life continued moving in a downward spiral, so that by the middle of winter I was indeed discovering the pain of being trampled underfoot.

One night I picked up a drunk from a bar who couldn't remember where he lived and filled my car with alcoholic fumes. Then I picked up a group of drunken, loud-mouthed football fans from a nightclub, who proceeded to vomit all over the back seat. After dropping them off, I cleaned it up as best I could, but the fare following gave me a mouthful of abuse and threatened to report me because of the foul smell.   Weary, depressed and very cold due to my unreliable heater, I pulled up for a break.

'This is hell on earth!' I voiced my thoughts aloud as I unscrewed my flask of tea. I opened my sandwiches but the smell of vomit inside the cab turned my stomach and I threw them back into the box. Opening the cab door I stepped outside. An icy blast cut through my coat but at least it was fresher than the air inside. I stamped my feet to keep warm and blew on my hands to bring feeling back into my fingers. My thoughts drifted to Eva and the children.

When I had my one day off a week I went to see them but it was always such a terrible wrench leaving them in the evening. Rae cried, Eva always tried to be brave and I always tried to be reassuring, but it was all one big act. Sometimes I missed seeing them altogether if I was asked to work overtime. Of course I was thankful for the extra money, but I was conscious that our present lifestyle couldn't go on like this for much longer.

'Oh God! Where is this going to end?'

Somewhere down an alley a dustbin clattered and a cat miaowed pitifully. A great wave of depression surged through me. What was I thinking earlier about a guardian angel looking after me? Well, where was he now? What good was this experience of taxi driving doing me? It was the most dead-end, useless job I'd ever been in! I needed a proper job. A job where I could come home every night, have a meal, play with my kids and see them off to bed. A job that wasn't continual night shift. Where I could have weekends and daylight and a few hobbies and friends. Was that too much to ask? All I was doing was sleeping, working, sleeping, working!

'If you're such a great God of love, then where's your love for me and Eva and the children?' I shouted to the empty streets. 'I need a daytime job! I need my home and family! I need . . . oh God!' My voice echoed down the empty alley-ways. No one heard. God didn't hear, but then

I didn't expect him to. I reckoned he'd left me when I walked out on him.

Cold and hungry and crying deep inside my soul, I climbed back into my foul-smelling cab and wound up the window. Pushing the key into the ignition, I was just about to start the engine when the thought came to me, 'Why don't you go and talk to Ray Gray? He's always given you good advice in the past.' I turned the key and the engine roared into life. That wasn't a bad idea. I would see Ray Gray. Winding down my windows so the icy blast tore through my cab, I continued on to my next fare but I didn't feel quite so bad. Somewhere, deep inside me, I had an aim.

Ray Gray wasn't surprised to see me. Instead he was quite annoyed that I hadn't called on him earlier. He had been the one to introduce me to boys' club work and training after demob and was upset by the way events had turned out at Alnmouth.

'I heard you were working somewhere in Newcastle, Alex. What are you doing?'

'Taxi driving, Ray.'

He nodded, shuffled in his seat and lowered his eyes, obviously uncomfortable about something. 'I'm really sorry to hear how events at the boys' club affected you and Eva. She's at her mam's house, is she?'

'Aye, she is. It's not been much of a life these last few months, Ray.'

'I can imagine. No chance of a reconciliation?'

I blinked rapidly. 'A what?'

'You and her getting back together again.'

I stared at him, horrified. 'We're not separated by choice, Ray. What gave you that idea?'

He looked duly embarrassed. 'I'm sorry. Really sorry, Alex. I heard on the grapevine that you were living with your parents again and that she'd gone back to live with hers. I guess I jumped to the wrong conclusion.'

I shook my head. 'I'd give anything for us to be back together again as a family, but I'm not earning enough.'

Ray paused for a moment, then he said, 'Have you ever thought of working in the city as a Child Care Officer, Alex?'

Memories flooded back of the first course of training I'd taken for the approved school when I'd listened to lectures by a Child Care Officer. But Roy's words didn't stir any enthusiasm in me at all. 'No, I don't fancy that.'

'You're more experienced with kids than you are taxi driving.'

'Anything's more suited to me than taxi driving.' I shook my head. 'But I can't see myself doing a job like that.'

'Well, if you change your mind let me know. I might be able to help.'

Whilst I said no, in the week that followed the idea wouldn't go away. That, coupled with driving on icy roads, persuaded me to at least see if there were any jobs available. There were! And so I moved into a job that I later discovered was really and truly tailor-made for me. A job I loved doing. A job that brought me into contact with homeless, vulnerable youngsters. I had a knowledge of Newcastle and the district that nobody else had. I knew all the seedy, low-life places the youngsters would go and the cafes they haunted.

It didn't occur to me to thank God for that knowledge that had come about through driving taxis. That was coincidence. It didn't occur to me to thank him for finding me a job that was a natural follow-up from what I'd done as a housemaster and youth leader. Ray Gray had done that! And it didn't occur to me to thank God for bringing my family back to me again. I'd done that all by myself!

135

ca 15 so

As a Child Care Officer one of my case-loads was Robert,
the youngest of a large family of brothers and half-sisters.
At sixteen Robert was a habitual criminal. The only good
thing I could say about him was that he had a great sense of
humour and a love of the outdoors. It was the latter that
decided me to encourage him to join the ship Arathusela
where he learned about seamanship and developed
leadership skills. Typically I heard very little from him
while he was with the Arathusela but a couple of weeks
before Christmas a call came through informing me that
Robert was home on leave and had refused to return to the
ship. I decided it would be best to visit the family and
headed towards one of the less salubrious parts of the city
where by chance I spotted Robert's tall, slim, dark-haired
figure swaggering slowly past the shops in a black leather
jacket. I pulled in at the kerb and wound down the window.

'Robert! Hey Robert!'

He turned and a broad grin spread across his face when he
saw who it was. 'Hi there, Mr Annand.' He glanced
around him. 'Better watch what you're doing in this area.
Wouldn't have thought you'd have needed a bit of the . . .'
He indicated to one of the local girls selling her 'wares' in a
shop doorway.

'Robert, we need to talk.'

He continued walking along the side of the kerb. 'Nothing
to talk about.'

I put my foot on the accelerator and kept pace with him.
'Yes there is, Robert. Why haven't you returned to the
Arathusela?'

'Didn't want to.'

'They're expecting you.'

'Get stuffed.'

I sighed. 'Get in the car, Robert, and we'll discuss this as I run you home.'

'Not going home.' He gave me a saucy wink. 'D' you not fancy any of these lasses?'

'You're joking!'

'You shouldn't be kerb-crawling along like that, Mr Annand. Better watch it. The cops'll have you.'

'Then get in the car and we can talk about it as I run you home.'

'Come on, Mr Annand! Not here! Me mates'll see.' He glanced around furtively, shoved his hands in his pockets and straightened his shoulders in an attempt to retain his street credibility. Obviously deciding he'd lost it anyway, talking to me, he made a sudden dart down one of the side alleys.

'Robert! Robert! Drat!' I stopped the car and hit the steering wheel in frustration. Now I'd have to spend all tomorrow hovering around the boxing club. I'd introduced Robert to boxing not long after I'd met him and was thrilled when he'd asked me to come and watch him in his first fight.

'Only when you come, tell me mates you're me da. OK?'

To actually get that type of breakthrough of acceptance from a lad like Robert made my job worthwhile, except when there were setbacks, like now.

There was a tap on the windscreen. I looked up in time to see a smirking traffic warden, with 'Got ya' written all over her face, slam a parking ticket under the windscreen wipers.

I returned home to find Eva fast asleep in front of the television. She stirred. 'You're late,' she murmured sleepily.

'Yes. Sorry, love. I forgot all about the time looking out for one of my kids.'

'Mmm. Well, one of your own kids was looking out for you all evening. Rae wants to remind you to come to see her in the Christmas play.'

'The Christmas play? Oh, right!'

She uncurled her legs and still yawning rose out of the chair. 'Don't forget it's tomorrow. Saturday. It's important to her.'

'No, no, I won't forget and I'm sorry I'm late, love.'

'Don't apologise to me. It's Rae and Iain who were upset they didn't see their dad before bedtime. I'm quite used to expecting you when I see you. I'll get your tea or supper, or whatever you want to call it.'

I sank down wearily into the vacated chair and stared glassy-eyed at the television droning on in the corner. We had a comfortable home in a town twenty miles away from the city centre. The children were happy at their school, Eva appeared to be contented with the area and the friends she'd made at the local church and my advancement in child care work had brought me deep satisfaction. The main problem was that while I spent my time wrapped up in my work, dealing with the problems of other children, it was often at the expense of not seeing my own two kids, and every now and then, like tonight, I felt the odd pang of guilt. Tiredness must have weighed heavier than the guilt on my mind, however, because I fell asleep. When I woke up my dinner had gone cold on the tray in front of me and Eva had gone to bed.

The following day, Saturday, I went to Robert's home. I had taken a real liking to this big, boisterous family, despite their rough ways. Robert's mother was a friendly, blowsy barmaid with a raucous laugh to go with her sense of humour but an iron will which kept her drunken husband and lively children more or less on the straight and narrow. The family were having a fry-up when I arrived, crowded around a big kitchen table.

'Sorry to interrupt you,' I apologised, hovering in the doorway.

'No problem!' I was assured. 'Sit yourself down, Mr Annand. Here, you lot! Move!' Robert's mother manoeuvred her brood around the table to leave a space for me.

'There's no need to go to all this trouble,' I started.

'Beer, Mr Annand?' Robert's father didn't wait for a reply but poured me a large glass of beer.

'We've spent all morning looking for our Robert,' his nineteen year old brother broke in. 'You had any luck?'

'Afraid not . . . no, please, Mrs er . . .' A warmed plate was pushed in front of me and a portion of fry-up taken from all seven plates around the table and deposited on to mine.

'Go on, eat up. I'm sorry our Robert's put you to all this bother. I'll skin the rotten **** alive when I get my hands on 'im!'

'Just let me know when you see him, Mrs Sampson, OK?'

'I'll do that, Mr Annand, and thanks. You've no idea how much we appreciate all you've done for 'im. We're in your debt.'

I laughed, embarrassed, and after clearing my plate – it would have been bad manners to do anything less – I left the house whistling happily, warmed by the meal, friendship and praise.

A little later, after visiting a few other houses in the area, I was about to drive off when one of Robert's brothers knocked on the car window. 'Glad I've caught you, Mr Annand. Mam said to tell you Robert's at the nick! He's been arrested for burglary.'

I didn't waste any time. I sped off in the direction of the local police station where the streetwise kid sat chewing gum in the interview room.

'Reckon I'll cop it this time, eh, Mr Annand?' He laughed nervously.

'Yes, I reckon you will, Robert,' I said nervously.

'Aye, well, never mind, eh?'

The happy-go-lucky attitude didn't fool me. I knew I had a very scared young lad on my hands. We sat talking for a while until his parents arrived. I did my best to reassure them and with promises to visit them at home on Monday, left Robert to talk to them. It was late afternoon by the time I arrived home. I opened the front door whistling cheerfully, expecting the usual greeting, and was surprised to find the house empty.

'Hello? Eva?' Puzzled, I wandered into the kitchen. All the note on the table said was 'Christmas Play'. It was enough to propel me hurriedly out of the house and down to the local church where I crept into the back of the darkened hall without being seen. Rae was already on stage with a tea towel draped around her head and a pet lamb in her arms. 'We have come to see the baby Jesus.' Her young voice rang out across the hall and her eyes flickered nervously towards the audience. 'We bring him our gifts.'

Halfway down the hall I saw Eva mouthing the words alongside her. While Rae and the other two shepherds were otherwise occupied depositing their gifts by the manger, I tiptoed up the aisle and sat on the seat Eva had kept for me.

'You're late!' she reproved, her eyes still glued to the stage.

'Sorry, love,' I whispered.

'Well, at least you're here now. Make sure Rae sees you.'

I embarrassed Eva, but made sure Rae and Iain saw me by leading a standing ovation at the end of the play.

'Did you enjoy me, dad?' Rae's bright face, coloured by stage make-up, looked up at me anxiously.

'Enjoy you? You were by far the best actress there, my love.'

'Did you see the curtains open and shut, dad? That was me!' Iain waited for his praise.

'Very professionally done, son. I thoroughly enjoyed the whole afternoon.'

Eva, standing beside me, gave a quiet snort. 'At least we've a lift home,' was all she said.

The excited chatter continued in the car all the way home.

'And don't forget we're all going carol singing on Christmas Eve, dad.' Rae watched my face anxiously. 'You are coming, aren't you?'

'Carol singing!' I'd forgotten all about it. In fact I'd almost forgotten about Christmas, I'd been so involved with my work. I glanced at Eva.

'You did promise, Alex,' she said quietly.

'Aye. OK. I'll be there.' Rae smiled happily and gave her brother a dig. 'See! I told you he'd come!'

How on earth had I managed to get myself embroiled in carol singing? On reflection it hadn't been too difficult.

'We're not going to church if you're not, dad!' My rebellious children had made that demand a couple of years ago and since then I'd usually managed to attend spasmodically. Of course it was always a good excuse when I was on call or at the duty office.

Over the next few days I placed Robert on the back-burner, as it were. His court case wasn't to be heard till January so he returned home on bail for Christmas. I spent the remaining days leading up to the holidays tidying up loose ends in the office and attending various functions.

'Les wondered if you'd like to go to the Christmas Eve service after we've been carol singing, Alex?'

Les and his wife attended the local church and had become good friends of ours.

'I don't know, Eva. Let's wait and see.' As I washed the dishes she was drying and putting away. 'In the last two weeks I've heard two sermons, seen one nativity play, been to one school carol service and on Christmas Eve I'll be carol singing. I don't think that's too bad a record, do you?'

'Depends on how much good it's doing you.'

I felt suddenly agitated with her. 'I've been down that road before, Eva, and I've no mind to go down it again!'

'Calm yourself. I'm not asking you to,' she said, returning a badly-washed dish to the sink again. 'I'm only passing on Les's message.'

It would have been a bit churlish to say no to Les, so that was why, after we'd been carol singing, I found myself sitting next to him, listening to my third sermon in two weeks. It was a warm, comfortable church and the friends we'd made here were likeable folk. The children in the Sunday school had decorated a Christmas tree and tiny white lights glistened in its dark green branches. Red candles flickered on the window-sills, bright against the dark panes of glass, and Christmas cards, sending best wishes to friends, filled the walls. I knew Eva would have sent one from us. She was good at seeing to things like that.

I can't remember what the address was; my mind was in other places. 'So we come to the time in the service when we share together in the breaking of bread and wine, symbolising our unity in Christ Jesus and remembering his sacrifice for us.'

I stirred from my wandering thoughts. I hadn't realised there'd be Communion.

'All those who love the Lord . . .'

The words were like the turning of a knife inside me.

' . . . are invited to share in the bread and wine.' The minister moved from the pulpit to the altar rail to administer Communion.

Love the Lord? I had loved him once and known him as a personal friend.

'NO!' The aggressor moved in and a battle began inside me. I deliberately focused my attention on the first section of the congregation who had moved forward to kneel at the altar to receive Communion. These friendly folk obviously loved Jesus. I could be one of them! This could be an opportunity for me to go forward and put things right with him.

'No! Don't be stupid!'

This might be the last chance I'd get.

'Stop thinking like that! Look what happened to you last time!'

I shuffled uneasily in my seat. A cold sweat came over me as the battle raged on inside my head. The steward continued moving silently up and down the aisles directing the people, the people who loved the Lord, to the Communion rail. The closer he came the greater the sense of panic that welled up inside me. I glanced at Les, sitting prayerfully beside me with his head bowed and his eyes closed. His whole body was relaxed and he had an expression of perfect peace across his face as he mentally prepared to go forward to receive the bread and wine.

'He's experiencing what I once had,' I thought sadly. The steward stopped at the end of our row and indicated that it was our turn to move forward for Communion if we wanted to take it. I didn't! Les got up, squeezed past me, and he and the others made their way to the altar at the front. I sat alone in the pew, listening to the organ softly playing carols in the background, watching the shadows from the candles flickering on the window-sills.

'Now is the time to come back to Me. Let go!' His voice was audible inside my head and I realised I hadn't experienced the warmth of his friendship for a long time. But then the aggressor was back. 'No! You'll get hurt again!'

The mental image of the peace on Les's face floated encouragingly through my mind. I wanted that peace! I did!

'Then let go. Let Jesus in!'

'No! You mustn't.'

'I want to.' I breathed a silent prayer of acceptance. 'I want to. I want him.'

It was as the final row of people were going forward for Communion that I knew it had to be now or never. So in that quiet, comfortable Methodist church on Christmas Eve, with the colourful Christmas cards, candles and with the organ playing carols, I leapt to my feet and clattered down the aisle to the Communion rail, squeezing in next to Les. Faces looked up, surprised, and smiled at me encouragingly. As I lifted my hands to receive the bread I gave my life back to Christ, and as I drank the wine I just knew that everything was going to be all right this time. At long last I had come to that perfect peace which is beyond all our understanding.

ᘓ 16 ᘔ

The juvenile court was hot, stuffy and crammed full of anxious parents, young people, probation officers and court officials. I found a quiet seat in the corner and withdrew a folder from my briefcase with the intention of glancing over the notes on Robert and his family before their case came up.

'Mr Annand?' One of the ushers called from across the corridor.

'Yes?'

'A quick word, if you don't mind.'

We discussed the case for a few minutes, then as soon as he'd left I pored over my file again.

'Alex Annand?'

'Yes.' Impatiently I covered my notes and looked up to see an enormous policeman, sporting three stripes, towering over me.

'I heard your name being called so I thought I'd come and have a word with the blue-eyed boy of the West End.'

'Pardon?'

The sergeant grinned warmly as he pulled a chair alongside mine.

'Sergeant Bill Nicholson.' He reached out an enormous hand and shook mine so hard that I swear I heard my teeth chatter. 'Made quite a name for yourself around young Robert's neck of the woods.'

It was quite a novel experience being referred to as a blue-eyed boy and I was only too pleased that Eva and my mother weren't around to put him right. I closed my folder and pocketed my pen, wondering what it was all about.

'You'll be here for young Robert?' he said, removing his helmet.

'That's right.'

He nodded. 'So you'll know Katie Sampson, his mother. Works at the bar down the High Street.

'Yes.'

'Uh-huh,' he paused thoughtfully. 'Perhaps you'll be interested in an incident we had there a couple of nights ago.'

'Incident?'

He waited until a couple of teenagers had moved out of earshot. 'Apparently Katie was serving behind the bar when she overhead a couple of chaps mention your name. One was Stan Toward and the other his mate, Percy Stamp. Know them?'

For a moment the names didn't register, but then the image of pot-bellied Stan who worked down at the market and his weasel mate, Percy, came into my mind. It wasn't a pleasant memory. Some months previously I'd been called in to assess whether Percy's children were at risk. Percy had gambled the money for the electricity bill on a 'sure winner' which turned out to be not quite the certainty he thought it was. He wasn't unduly perturbed, however, as he assumed that if his children were considered at risk Social Services would pay his bills. Unfortunately, as I reported that his children were not at risk, he was left to raise the money the best way he could, but not before ensuring I received a mouthful of abuse for placing him in such a predicament.

'Yes, I know Percy and Stan,' I said to Sergeant Nicholson. 'Right couple of . . . characters.'

The sergeant nodded his head in agreement. 'Well, apparently Katie overheard Percy slagging you off to Stan for not agreeing to pay his electricity bill and threatening to duff you up in the car park one night, just to teach you a lesson.'

I shuffled uncomfortably. I didn't like the sound of this.

'Fortunately, Katie's always one for looking after her own interests and with you doing so much for young Robert, you must have come under the heading of "Katie's interests".' Anyway, she went round the back of the bar where two of her sons were humping crates and told them what she'd overheard. A few minutes later, according to my source, the Sampson boys well . . . shall we say they escorted Percy and Stan out of the bar by the scruff of their necks and left them in no doubt as to what would happen if they so much as laid a finger on you.' The sergeant chuckled. 'They're a rough bunch, the Sampsons, but you've certainly wound your way into their family.'

'So you don't think Percy and Stan are out to teach me a lesson any more?'

The sergeant shook his head. 'I doubt it. I shouldn't think you'll have any trouble, but it wouldn't do any harm to keep your eyes and ears peeled for a while.'

'I'll do that. Thanks for the warning.'

I didn't have time to get worked up over Stan and Percy at that moment as my name was called and my time taken up with the court case in hand. It didn't take long; Robert was sent to Borstal.

'It isn't fair!' Katie Sampson burst into tears. Her husband frowned worriedly and the older Sampson boys solemnly contemplated the verdict. As Robert made to leave the court under police escort he turned to me with his usual cheery grin.

'Aye, well, I've had a good run for my money, I suppose. Never mind, Mr Annand. Not even you could have got me off this one.'

I gave him a reassuring pat on the shoulder as he made his way out of the court, handcuffed to a policeman.

147

Robert's case had a profound effect on his family. His mother kept his photograph on the mantelpiece in her living room as a constant warning to her younger sons of the penalty of crime, and I continued to call in on the family from time to time, helping to reinforce Katie Sampson's attempts to keep crime from her doors.

I took Sergeant Nicholson's advice and kept my ears and eyes open, avoiding the market and street where Percy and Stan lived and worked. I wasn't over-anxious to bump into them or their thugs. I knew I was no match for them. So, much to Eva's amazement, I was home for tea early every night for the next few weeks.

'What's wrong?' she asked, puzzled.

'Nowt! Can I not come early to see my wife and bairns if I've a mind?'

She eyed me suspiciously. 'Mmm. I don't believe that for one minute.'

I grinned. 'Eva! Fancy being suspicious of your own husband. If I were late you'd be suspecting another woman.'

'No, I wouldn't! No one in their right mind would put up with you so I've no worries on that score! Give over, Alex!' she giggled as I grabbed the strings of her pinny. 'Not in front of the children!'

I did my best to keep my unease from Eva and the children, hoping that in time Stan and Percy would either let bygones be bygones or feel threatened enough by the Sampsons to leave me alone. Nevertheless this type of tension didn't do anything for my nerves and was partly responsible for me applying for a job in a smaller authority which appeared to have greater career prospects than my present position. I was appointed court officer, liaising with courts, social workers, police and remand homes. But I'd hardly got my feet under the desk, so to speak, before a reshuffle in local boundaries meant a change for everyone in Local

Government. Anxiously I waited to see if, once again, I would be joining the ranks of the unemployed.

A few days before our annual summer holiday I had an interview for a post in the new, larger Social Services Department. Eva and I waited nervously for the postman each morning, wondering if we'd done the right thing in planning a holiday away at this time. No letter came and we spent an anxious holiday wondering about our future again. At the end of the week I returned to work to find out what was happening. I was sorting through the papers on my desk when Mrs Parsons, our tea lady, came up behind me.

'Tea, Alex?'

'Please.'

'Two sugars, isn't it?'

'Yes, thanks.'

'There you are, love, and by the way, congratulations on your new appointment.'

That was how I discovered I was to be the advisor to residential homes in the authority because of my residential experience.

The next few weeks in my new job were extremely stressful. We hadn't had much of a holiday because of worries about unemployment again and I was feeling rather run down from a nasty bout of flu. Matters weren't made any better when I had a telephone call from one of my ex-colleagues to say that John, a lad of eighteen who had been in my care for a few years, had been arrested.

'Arrested what for?' I asked. There was silence at the other end of the telephone.

'For pity's sake, Harry. The lad was in my care for three years!'

'Murder.'

'Murder?' My hand gripped the telephone tightly. 'What happened?'

'Well, it's difficult to say.' I was aware that he was bound by confidences.

'There's not a lot to tell, Alex. As you know we've suspected John's stepfather of sexually abusing his stepsister, but there's never been enough proof for us to do anything, so from what I gather, John decided to take matters into his own hands.'

My heart went out to this young lad. He wasn't a bad kid and may have stood a fair chance in society if his home life hadn't been fraught with violence. But murder! I would never have thought him capable of such an aggressive act.

'We need to meet,' Harry went on. 'My director has spoken to yours and they've agreed to me meeting with you since you've been involved with John over a longer period of time than I have. I need to make sure nothing's been missed when I prepare the report for court.'

'What do you mean, you need to make sure nothing's been missed?' My fingers tightened again on the telephone.

'Could we have done more about the abuse, things like that.'

'But nothing was proved.' I could feel the muscles in my stomach tightening. Was Harry suggesting I hadn't done my job properly?

'No use worrying, Alex,' he said. 'What's done's done.'

Anxiously I replaced the receiver. Was there anything I could have done to prevent John from getting to the point where he felt that murder was the only option?

Over the following few weeks I discovered to my disappointment that the position didn't in practice have the powers of authority I'd been led to expect, and that my reports were seldom, if ever, acted on. After making discreet enquiries I discovered that other irregularities were taking place. Nothing serious or criminal, but I was disturbed enough to start keeping a personal copy of all my reports, just to cover myself.

I had a quiet word with my immediate superior but nothing changed, and I decided a formal complaint was in order. But the more I complained, the more difficult life at work was made for me. In fact all manner of petty complaints began to be levelled in my direction about the standard of my work, none of which stood up to scrutiny. Working with my colleagues in an atmosphere of mistrust, struggling to cope with the pressures of the job, trying to dispel pangs of guilt that I could have done more for John, and worries over the reports I'd made regarding his home situation, wasn't doing my blood pressure any good. Gradually the stress and tension began to tell and I found it all too easy to snap at Eva and the children.

Finally, confrontation came when I was called in to see my boss at the end of one afternoon. 'Come in.' He opened the door, checked to make sure nobody was in the immediate vicinity, then closing the door he turned and snapped: 'A warning, Annand! Keep pushing and it'll cost you your job!'

My temper rose quickly. 'If that's your attitude I'm off to see my union rep, but before I go I'd like to know why you didn't act on my last report? What's the good of me making reports if you don't act on them?' I hadn't meant to make such a loud outburst, but I felt goaded by his attitude.

He was a man who had been in Local Government for a long time. Starting as a clerk he'd worked his way up the ladder to his now senior position as administrator. He had no professional experience or qualifications as a social worker, working mainly in administration, and this loud outburst did nothing to improve his opinion of me. He raised his eyebrows questioningly as he made his way round to the other side of the desk and sat down. 'And which report is that?' he asked smoothly.

'My recommendation for dismissal of the woman caught stealing.'

'Ah, yes. I read it.' He shuffled some papers on his desk.

'Then why on earth was she allowed to be employed in a new home without the matron being informed of all the circumstances?' I snapped.

He eyed me coldly. 'That is none of your concern.'

'If it's none of my concern then what the blazes am I doing making recommendations which you have no intention of following?' I demanded.

'I don't think I like your tone, Mr Annand.'

'And I don't like this bloody system you've got here. If you ask me . . .'

'I'm not asking you!'

'I want to know what you're going to do . . !'

He stood up. 'Mr Annand. Let's get one thing clear. You make your reports. It's none of your business what I see fit to do with those reports.'

'Well, that's fine by me!' I bellowed. 'But you'd better know I'm keeping a copy of all the reports and recommendations I send through this office, because I'm not carrying the can if things go wrong! The system you've got here sounds very underhand to me!' I could have kicked myself for mentioning my private reports. Me and my big mouth!

'Underhand?' my supervisor spat. 'Underhand? Nothing we do in this office is underhand!'

'Isn't it? Hasn't one of your lackeys downstairs been checking up on me?'

He didn't answer.

'He has, hasn't he?' I shouted.

He blinked rapidly.

'I'm warning you,' I threatened, 'I'll take this matter further if I have to.'

The silent hostility that had grown between us during this encounter suddenly erupted. I hurled a tirade of abuse at him, then turning abruptly on my heel, stormed out of his office, slamming the door after me. By the time I'd grabbed my coat and briefcase and made my way down to the dark, empty car park I was shaking like a leaf. I took a deep breath, trying to steady my nerves, reached into my pocket and took out a packet of cigarettes. Smoking was a habit I'd developed some years ago and it had increased in recent weeks due to the stress I'd been under.

'It would be me that would cop it if anything started to go wrong!' I muttered, skirting a deep pothole full of water. It had been raining all day, leaving puddles everywhere. Rummaging for my keys as I walked, I made my way to the car. Agitatedly I opened the door and slid into the driver's seat.

'I can't win whichever way I turn. He's a smarmy ****!' I started the engine and revved up angrily. 'He's nothing more than a . . .' I took a deep breath in an attempt to calm down before I drove home, ' . . . patronising son of a ****!'

There was a loud noise, like the sound of a firecracker, from the engine followed by a pungent smell of petrol and burning, then a sudden explosion rocked the car and thick black smoke billowed from under the bonnet. Panic-stricken I struggled to unfasten my seat-belt. Somewhere in the car park a voice yelled, 'Get out! Get out, Alex!' and the next moment the car door was flung open. I dived out of the car, flung myself on to the wet tarmac and rolled over a few times till I was sure I was clear. I landed in one of the potholes. There was a hissing noise. Glancing up I saw one of my colleagues standing over the bonnet of my car with the office fire extinguisher. Shakily I got to my feet and surveyed the blackened bonnet.

'You OK, Alex?'

'Yes. Yes, I'm OK,' I said shakily. 'What happened?'

My colleagues shook his head. 'Dunno, I'm sure, but you're lucky. If it had caught the petrol tank . . .' He shook his head, leaving the sentence unfinished.

For the next few weeks I had an extra hour or so added to my day by having a tiresome journey to and from work by bus until my car was fixed. I arrived at work one morning to be handed a bill by one of the senior clerks. 'You weren't given authority to use a fire extinguisher,' he said bluntly, 'and it has to be paid for.'

I stared at him in amazement. 'You're having me on?'

He shook his head.

'In that case,' I snapped, 'give it to the person who used it on my car which was about to explode, because I'm not paying for it!'

'You'll have to pay for it or it'll be taken off your wage.'

'You touch my wage and you'll really be in trouble,' I warned.

'Then I'll have to see the boss,' he said stubbornly.

'You see who you want! I'm not paying for it and that's final!' I stormed out of the office and went upstairs to see the colleague who had used the extinguisher.

'Tell you what,' he said. 'Let's go and see the union rep.'

That was the last I heard of the matter but the following day Harry arrived to give me the latest news of John. He had been sentenced to twelve years' imprisonment for the murder of his stepfather. Twelve years! As his supervising officer at the time, surely I should have spotted that something was amiss? Was I to blame in any way? I worried that my mind was starting to go. So many people seemed to have it in for me, I even began to wonder if the fire in the car had been a deliberate action, until I received a call from the RAC.

'The tube that feeds the petrol to the engine split. Petrol on your hot engine caused it to ignite.'

At least it was a pure accident but it was just one more stress to add to all the others. I had always tried to give of my best, and taken a pride in my work. Now I was faced with innuendo after innuendo suggesting I wasn't capable of doing my job, and a bill for the fire extinguisher, with worries over John and continually having to work in an atmosphere of distrust. I didn't know how much more I could take.

A few days later I returned home one night with a tight band across my chest which seemed to restrict my breathing. I also had a thumping headache. I opened the front door, struggling to fight off the waves of nausea which threatened to engulf me, and just had time to rush to the toilet where I was violently sick.

Nervous exhaustion, the doctor said. Where was God in this?

'Rest, Alex. The doctor said rest!' Eva didn't usually lay down the law and I was finding it increasingly annoying that she'd chosen to do so now. She stood with her hands on her hips, surveying me angrily.

'Aye! Well, I'm resting! I'm resting!'

'No, you're not, Alex. You're standing on a chair rummaging through those cupboards. Dragging out walking boots, haversack and the football doesn't look like resting to me!'

'Oh, Eva, give over!' I stuck my head further into the cupboard to hide my guilt. 'Ah! Found it!' Gleefully I pulled out the sleeping bag.

'Honestly, Alex! You're hopeless! A weekend camping with the Boys' Brigade is hardly restful for someone who's been on the verge of a nervous breakdown.'

'I'm bored, Eva. I've been off work for weeks now. Anyway, I'm loads better and well enough to start the new job next week. Don't fuss so.'

'Don't fuss! I'm the one who'll have to pick up the pieces if your nerves get shot again!'

Fortunately I was rescued at that moment by a knock on the door. 'Hello? Anyone home?'

'Aye, Les. Come on in. You've just saved me from a fate worse than death.'

'Oh?'

'Aye. Eva's tongue. How about a cuppa for a sick man and his pal, my pet.'

'Sick man! You've got a nerve!' She glowered in my direction then rolled her eyes helplessly towards Les. 'Can't do a thing with him, Les. He's determined to have this weekend away.' She headed towards the kitchen and Les, looking decidedly guilty, made for the chair in the corner.

'Are you sure about this weekend?' he asked warily, eyeing the kitchen door. 'I don't want you overdoing it.'

'Certain, Les. I'm not one for acting the invalid. A weekend away'll do me the world of good and give me the chance to spend some time with our Iain.' In fact Iain was one of my main reasons for agreeing to help Les out at this Boys' Brigade camping trip. It seemed as if my son was growing up fast and I'd hardly paid heed to what he was up to or how he was developing. At least being at home for the last few weeks had forced me to slow down and take stock of what my children were doing and where I was headed in life. I'd finally made the decision to tender my resignation, when out of the blue I was actually offered a job with my previous local authority where I'd been so happy. It was a sideways promotion, but I looked forward to returning to work with them.

'I really do appreciate your offer to help, Alex,' Les said gratefully.

That was how I found myself standing in the corner of the field late one summer's afternoon absorbing what warmth was left in the sun, turning sizzling sausages over a barbecue and trying to keep track of a game of football at the far end of the field, where excited yells informed me that Iain's team was winning. A sausage fell through to the charcoal and hot cinders warmed my face as I bent to retrieve it. I was finding simple mundane tasks incredibly relaxing. Whistling quietly I prepared the boys' supper, my mind running over the short talk Les had asked me to give for the epilogue that night.

More cheers and shouts from the football pitch informed me that the game was over and twenty-odd muddy footballers descended upon me, or rather upon their supper. That evening we gathered around the camp fire for the usual singsong and epilogue. Iain eyed me suspiciously. He'd never seen his dad in this sort of role before and was obviously unsure what to make of it, especially when I threw myself wholeheartedly into the story I'd prepared and captured the attention of the boys so effectively.

'Great stuff, Alex,' Les commented as we cleared up for the night. 'You had them eating out of your hand. Didn't know you could spout forth like that.'

I laughed, embarrassed. 'Neither did I,' I said, pleased by his praise. 'Full of hidden talents, that's me.'

Les threw some soil over the glowing embers of the camp fire and said thoughtfully, 'Have you ever thought of being a preacher?' The words seemed to hang, poised in the air, waiting to see what my reaction would be.

Thought about it? Of course I'd thought about it. Twenty-odd years ago I'd thought of little else but my calling to be a minister and preach the gospel in the Anglican Church. Aggressively I threw another handful of soil on the fire. There was still a lot of hurt, confusion and disappointment every time I thought about the failure of those years. It seemed that deep inner pain was never very far from the surface.

'Have you?' Les stooped to retrieve an abandoned sock as we made our way back to our tent under the dark starlit sky.

'What? Thought about preaching?' I hesitated. 'Not recently, no.'

'My opinion, for what it's worth, is that you ought to think seriously about it, Alex.' He disappeared inside the tent and I heard him clattering about as he got ready for bed, but I wasn't ready for sleep. I was suddenly restless. Old memories had been stirred up by Les's comment and I needed space to think.

Although it was dark, there was still enough light from the moon to see my way down to the river. Quietly I passed tents full of flashing torches, midnight feasts, giggles and loud 'Ssshhhs' as I headed for the river bank. I stood for a long time watching the river sparkling under the full moon, trickling its way to the estuary. It was quiet down here, away from the camp. The wind whispered through the trees and the odd call of a night owl and the bleating of sheep in the hills seemed to awaken a sense of a God of nature that had been dormant inside me for a long time. I realised how little time I actually spent standing still, listening or finding any sense of peace. I always seemed to be so busy, my whole life geared to one mad rush. What was it someone had said to me once? 'Do you ever stand still or remain quiet long enough for God to speak to you, Alex?' Perhaps he'd never stopped calling me to preach his Word. Perhaps it had never really left me but just got lost along the way when I'd turned my back and stopped listening to the One who was doing the calling. I took a deep breath. The smell of charred wood from the bonfire drifted in my direction.

'So,' I prayed softly. 'You want to call me into local preaching, do you?' I stood for a long time, thoughtfully contemplating before I said, 'OK, then.'

But every morning after my return home, I would look at myself in the mirror with my face covered in shaving foam and shake my head. No matter how hard I tried I could not visualise myself in the pulpit. I wasn't conventional Methodist preacher-type material. On top of which those old deep hurts of rejection and failure kept rearing their ugly heads to haunt me and with them came new fears, that once again I might be moulded into someone else's idea of a preacher, or that I would be unable to match up to the expectations of others. These things weighed heavily on me as well as concerns over my quick temper, heavy smoking and my continual need to swear. But the feeling I had about being called to preach persisted, and in the end I went to have a word with our local minister.

'Come on in, Alex. Nice to see you.' Revd Gunn was a wise, elderly man who greeted me warmly as he opened the manse door. A big, black, overweight Labrador bounded up in greeting.

'Sit yourself down,' he said. I think he was talking to me, not the dog. 'Been a lovely day, hasn't it?' He removed a half-knitted jumper from the chair and carefully draped it over one of the china cabinets. 'We haven't bothered with a coal fire tonight. Hope you'll be warm enough while we chat.' He turned on one bar of the electric fire to take the chill off the room then sat opposite me. The Labrador curled up between my feet and the fire. 'Now then, what can I do for you?'

Despite years of social work experience in dealing with all sorts of people, I found I was decidedly nervous. How could I, with all my faults and bad habits, approach this fine Christian man and ask him to consider my request to preach? I was not only asking for trouble, I was asking for more rejection!

'Well, I've . . . er . . . been thinking, er . . .' I stammered and he raised his eyebrows encouragingly. I took a deep breath. 'I've been wondering about preaching,' I blurted out.

His face lit up. 'That's wonderful, Alex. Wonderful! Tell me a bit more.'

His reaction so surprised and pleased me that, without going into too many details of my past, I found myself launching forth into a pretty accurate description of my weekend at the camp, including my reaction to Les's comment that I ought to preach the Gospel.

'The only trouble is, I have a slight problem,' I concluded.

'Most of our preachers do have a few problems when they start out, Alex.'

'Aye, but I bet none of them have the problem of swearing like a trooper, smoking like a chimney and a quick temper to boot!'

There! I'd said it! It was out in the open. He raised his eyebrows again and was about to speak but having got my concerns out into the open I was now in full flow. 'It's not as if I haven't prayed about these things and tried to stop. It's just impossible. Swearing was part of my lifestyle when I was growing up in the back streets of Aberdeen. We all swore, although not in front of the womenfolk. My dad wouldn't allow that. But outside, with my friends. Then when I joined the army it was a natural part of everyday language.' My mind flickered momentarily to Mick who'd managed to curtail the blasphemy around him. 'I don't take the Lord's Name in vain, not any more, and I don't use exceptionally foul language any more either, not since I became a Christian. It's the other cusses I can't get rid of, the smoking I can't stop and the temper that always flares when it shouldn't.' I dried up and dropped my eyes to my feet. I should have polished my shoes before I came but the Labrador appeared to be doing a pretty good job of licking off the scuff marks. 'I dunno what to do,' I concluded lamely. 'The call to preach is there but the swearing and stuff . . . I've tried and tried to stop, but the harder I try the more I swear.'

'Then stop trying, Alex.'

I looked up at him, surprised, and watched a broad grin spread across his face. 'If God is calling you to preach, simple things like swearing, smoking and your quick temper aren't going to cause him problems. You have two years to study and train as a local preacher and to put your calling to the test, and during that time he will equip you to do the work he has called you to do.'

The hairs on the back of my neck bristled. He hadn't equipped me when he'd called me before. I'd failed all my exams! Revd Gunn leant forward and, almost as though he was following my train of thought, said. 'If you've tried the best you know how and failed, then hand it over to God, Alex. He will do the rest. Teamwork!'

That made sense. If I was honest, I certainly hadn't given of my best in the past. I'd foolishly and naively believed that God would equip me for everything without putting everything into it myself.

'Give it to God,' I repeated.

'Tell you what I'll do, Alex. I'll put your name forward at the next local preachers' meeting to get you started, and we'll take it a step at a time. How does that sound?' 'So you don't think the swearing, smoking and the quick temper is too much of a problem?'

He shook his head. 'As long as you're not blaspheming in the pulpit, Alex. I think by the time we get you started you'll find yourself adapting to your new calling. What is it we sing in that hymn 'Love Divine'? Ah, yes. 'Changed from glory into glory.' Allow God to start those changes in you now, Alex.'

A wave of relief spread over me. 'You've certainly put my mind at rest.' I stood up, narrowly missing the dog's tail. 'Thanks a lot for the chat.' I shook his hand, firmly hoping I was showing the warmth and gratitude I was feeling, and a few minutes later, when the dog had let go of my trouser leg, I left his manse with a strange feeling in my guts that swearing at least, wouldn't be a problem.

It never was!

℃ **18** ℗

A trickle of rain ran down the back of my neck and under my collar. I hunched my shoulders, pulling my overcoat tighter in an attempt to keep out the coldest and wettest February weather for many years.

The other strikers, most of them qualified professional social workers, stood miserably around the Civic Centre like lost sheep, stamping their feet and blowing into their hands to keep warm. Being on the picket line was no fun! Initially, all the basic grade Social Workers wanted was an improvement in their pay conditions, but as soon as the word 'strike' was mentioned it seemed to be a signal for a handful of militants to emerge from out of the woodwork to take control. Suddenly, all sorts of side issues erupted. The strike was now into its fifth month and had escalated beyond all recognition, causing massive traffic jams throughout the city and great antagonism, from foul language to physical aggression, towards the bosses who were left to run the department. It had become an ugly strike, bringing out the worst and best in all of us.

I shivered and gazed glumly through the mist and rain towards colleagues reflecting my own misery and discomfort. A Ford Cortina pulled up in front of the gates, and the driver wound down his window, glared in disgust at us, then indicated with two fingers.

'Thank you, sir!' I wondered, not for the first time, what on earth I was doing here. As a senior Social Worker the dispute over pay conditions didn't personally affect me. But since I came from a family with strong socialist ideals and commitments to the union, I could do no other than give my support. However, the longer the strike lasted the more aggressive it became and I was finding it increasingly difficult to come to terms with the suffering and bad feeling it was causing.

I watched a tall, bearded man in a dog-collar approaching, his wide intellectual brow furrowed in creases.

'Good morning.' I smiled pleasantly as he approached, waiting for an agreeable response.

He came to an abrupt halt inches from the end of my nose. 'Don't you dare "good morning" me!' he spat. Alarmed, I stepped back. 'People like you don't give a toss for the suffering you're causing or the hardship you're inflicting.' His eyes blazed angrily into mine.

'And what do you know about suffering?' My smile froze but my easily roused temper remained strangely dormant.

He stood his ground as I removed frozen hands from my coat pockets but continued to glare angrily at me. 'I know I'm seeing poverty, hardship and depression, and uncaring people like you not doing a thing about it! Too wrapped up in wage claims and petty self-interest!'

'Really?' I could see one or two of my colleagues taking an interest in the exchange of words. 'People like me, huh? Well, it might surprise you to know that some of us here on strike are Christians and we care deeply about these things. What we don't need to add to our sufferings are your sanctimonious criticisms and aggressive attitudes. What we really need are your prayers that this strike will be resolved, quickly!'

He blinked rapidly and I enjoyed a surge of delight at having taken the wind out of his sails.

'And,' I continued, 'if you'd like to help us do something useful, instead of bellyaching, perhaps you could join us at Brunswick Methodist Church where you'll find a Christian lunchtime club run by the overworked wife of the minister and myself, to help folk with their problems.'

Tackling another Christian obviously wasn't what he'd bargained for. 'Yes, well, good for you! But the sooner you accept what's been offered by your employers, the better!' Abruptly he turned on his heel and walked swiftly down the street before I could think of a suitable retort.

'Sanctimonious ****.' I still hadn't stopped swearing completely but as I thrust my hands back into my pockets I was pleased at how calm I'd remained during the exchange of words. I glanced at my watch. A few more minutes and it would be time for me to go to the lunchtime club. One of the good things that had come out of this strike was not only an awareness of the needs of fellow strikers but the realisation that there were fellow Christians involved. So I had started impromptu counselling sessions which, with the help of Revd Geoff Clark's wife, had escalated into a Christian lunchtime club at the Methodist church in the city centre.

I moved my position from the gate to the pavement about six feet away, wondering if I'd find the sanctimonious dog-collar at the lunchtime club and vowed, there and then, that when I became a minister I'd make sure I didn't condemn and judge folk like myself. The ministry! I still found it hard to believe that come September I'd be at Queen's College, Birmingham, a student once more, and this time training for ordination into the Methodist Church.

It had all started when I'd returned to help Les with the Boys' Brigade camping trip the following year. There'd been something familiar and comforting about that weekend. The big field with the river running down the side, the tents in neat rows and the football pitch at the end. Even with thirty boys running riot it had a strangely relaxing effect. This was the place where God had called me to preach and here, exactly one year and one week later, another call came. A call into the ministry. The same call I'd heard almost twenty years ago. There was no sudden blinding flash or revelation, only a gradual awareness that God wanted more from me. This time I was more than a little cautious. If this was a genuine call from God then he would have to make it crystal-clear, because I was too afraid of heading off down the wrong path again.

'Lord,' I prayed, 'If you want me in the ministry, get someone to ask me outright.' No chance of any mistakes with a prayer like that!

The rich smell of pipe tobacco filling the warm evening air heralded the arrival of Les at the camp fire. 'They're in high spirits,' he said, nodding towards the lads clearing up after their supper.

'Aye. They are that.' I threw another log on to the crackling embers and we watched silently as sparks flew into the air.

'How's the studying for the local preaching going?' he asked after a while.

'Quite well. I'm halfway through. Hard work, though.'

'Mmm.' He sucked his pipe. 'And when you've finished, what then?'

'What do you mean?'

His next question just threw me. 'Have you given any thought to the ministry?'

I stared at him with my mouth open. For the first time in my life I was lost for words.

'It might be a good idea for you to think and pray about it,' he said.

I found my vocal chords. 'I don't believe you've just said that, Les.'

'Oh?' He removed his pipe and started the laborious task of relighting it. 'Why?'

'Because I prayed that . . .' I shook my head. 'It doesn't matter. What made you suggest the ministry?'

He gazed thoughtfully into the fire before answering. 'I believe it's your calling, Alex. Don't you?'

I shook my head in disbelief. 'Les, I don't know whether to kick you or hug you!' He backed away sharply and I began to relate my prayer to him. Then we stood in a companionable silence watching the flames dancing in the camp fire, listening to the chatter and laughter of the boys and smelling the rich aroma of Les's pipe.

'Alex! Alex!' I was quickly brought back to the misery of the picket line.

'Yes? Sorry. I was miles away. Janet, isn't it?'

The young chubby-faced girl with a plastic mac wrapped tightly around her wore a worried expression on her face. 'Yes. There's an urgent telephone call for you in the office, Alex . . .'

Even as I made my way inside the building I sensed something was wrong and instinctively braced myself for bad news. Since my father's stroke some months ago his condition had continued to give cause for concern. He'd turned angry, aggressive, even violent at times and I was constantly having to visit my parents' home to support my mother. Then a few weeks ago he'd been admitted into hospital to have his leg amputated.

'It's mother, Alex,' my sister Kathleen informed me from the other end of the telephone.

'Mother?'

'Yes. The General Hospital's telephoned to say she had a bad fall at home this morning and they're going to have to operate. I'm up at the hospital now.'

I didn't panic. Why panic? I just leapt into my car and drove like a lunatic through the city centre. 'Keep calm! Keep calm!' I told myself. 'It'll all work out.' I only had both my parents in different hospitals, my local preachers' final exam in two days, preparation for an entry exam and interview for the ministry next month, and I was on strike! Why worry?

Kathleen met me in the hospital corridor, white-faced and anxious. 'It was a nasty fall, Alex. I don't know what she was up to, clambering up ladders.' I took her elbow and we moved to an open window in a quiet part of the waiting room. Anxious though I was, the clinical smells and hospital atmosphere still triggered off unpleasant memories.

'What did the doctor say?'

Kathleen shook her head. 'Not a lot. All I know is, it's a very bad break to her ankle. She's been in the operating theatre for nearly four hours.'

'Four hours?' I scratched my chin anxiously. 'It doesn't look as though we'll be able to see her for some time. Shall I pop over to the other hospital and see dad? Perhaps you can hang on here?' Somehow we managed to formulate a plan of action to cover both hospitals and after wading back through the congested city I eventually arrived at my father's bedside.

His pale blue eyes were expressionless as they looked into mine. It was impossible to tell how much he fully understood what was going on. I was pretty sure he'd be wondering where mam was, but in his frail condition I hadn't the heart to tell him.

'Mam says she'll be in to see you in a day or so, dad. Caught the flu, so thought she'd better not come in here and pass it on.' Christian or not, I was still a pretty convincing liar. I patted his wrinkled hand reassuringly and wished Eva or Kathleen had been with me. It wasn't easy holding a one-way conversation. Since his stroke dad hadn't uttered a word, and it was distressing to watch his frustration as he tried to make himself understood. I readjusted his pillows, sadly aware of how the flesh had fallen from his stocky frame.

'Been picketing today, dad. In all this rain. Hope I don't catch the flu like mam, eh?' Was that a question in his eyes?

'Strike should be over soon, they reckon. A settlement's on the cards. Good, eh?' He nodded. Yes, that was a definite nod.

'Perhaps get you home soon, if you keep improving like this. Have to wait till mam's flu's gone, though.'

Yes. He looked pleased by that idea. Just a few words, dad. Just a few? But the doctor didn't seem to think he would ever speak again.

I stayed a while longer, struggling to keep up this one-way conversation, praying for a few words from dad, just a few. I desperately tried to read something into the odd flicker on his face and although my wave of farewell was cheerful, my heart felt like lead when I left. I was weighed down with love and concern for both my parents and guilty that I had kept the truth from dad. I wept inwardly on my way to the car park. 'God! Oh God, if only I could talk with my dad, just once more! If only I could tell him I was going into the ministry and hear him say, just once, that he was proud of me.' I gave way to tears of frustration inside the car. God and the world suddenly seemed cruel and unjust. A passer-by glanced curiously at me, but then hospitals were places for worried faces and tears. He walked on and I removed my glasses and wiped my eyes. After a while I calmed down. Then starting up the engine I returned to the General Hospital to see Kathleen and discover if mam was out of the operating theatre.

I surprised even myself with how I coped with the strike, visited my parents, and prepared for exams, ministerial interviews and preaching appointments. Normally I would have panicked and it would all have proved too much for me to cope with, but much to Eva's amazement I remained quite calm, and other than the odd restless night dreaming about failing exams, hospitals, broken ankles, strokes and amputations, Moses and the prophets, theology and the ethics of striking, I slept pretty well! At least being on strike gave me the opportunity to visit both hospitals. The doctors didn't appear to think there'd be any reason why mam shouldn't make a good recovery and return home in a few days but she would have to wear a caliper for the rest of her life.

Dad was quite another matter. He underwent a further amputation, this time above his knee and the days prior to the operation found him more weepy than usual. My own concern was whether or not he would survive a second operation but he did, and a few days later I walked into the ward where he lay. Despite tubes, drips and wires coming out of his body he looked better, and the pleasure of seeing me showed on his face.

'Hello, dad. How's it going then? You look a lot better. Doctor says you've had to have blood transfusions?'

He nodded his head, anxiously scanning my face as I sat down.

'Mam? She's loads better. We hope to bring her in to see you at the end of the week. That'll be nice, eh?' I racked my brains for more news. 'I sat my local preachers' exams a couple of days ago. That was why I missed coming in to see you, but I gather our Kathleen came in and so did Eva.'

His eyes certainly seemed brighter today. Yes, he was definitely looking better.

'And some news I've been going to tell you for a while now, dad. I've had confirmation from the Church that I've been accepted for training as a minister. That means I'll only be able to visit some weekends mind, dad. You won't forget me, will you?'

'No.'

At first it didn't register that the voice had come from the bed. 'I don't expect it'll take long to travel from . . . dad? You said . . .'

'I . . . won't . . . forget.' The croaked whisper through dried lips sent a shock wave through my whole system. He'd spoken! My father had spoken!

'How did you . . . when did you know you could speak, dad?'

It took a while for him to reply. 'Last night . . . after . . . you . . . left.'

I held his thin bony hand and looked deeply into his pain-filled eyes, realising I was seeing an answer to my prayers.

'Pleased . . . you're . . . going into the . . . ministry . . . son . . . Proud!'

The child in me, who had continually sought his approval throughout the years, glowed under his words of praise.

Amazingly and inexplicably, for seven days he was able to converse in short, incomplete sentences then, as quickly as his speech had returned, it went. When I spoke to the doctors about it they wouldn't commit themselves by giving any real explanation as to what had happened. Perhaps something to do with the blood they'd given him, they said, but I remembered my prayers to God, pleading for my father to speak, if only for a while before he died.

171

He had not only answered my prayer but given me my earthly father's approval for my move into the ministry.

I believe what happened was nothing short of a miracle.

⚝ 19 ⚝

I pulled in at a service station and parked at the rear of the building away from the noise and fumes of the motorway traffic. I stretched, easing muscles that had stiffened from the long drive south to Birmingham, then glanced at my watch. Another hour should do it. Turning to the flask of tea and sandwiches Eva had made for my break I tucked in hungrily, enjoying the rest and solitude of the car park. A few other travellers had stopped with the same idea in mind but my corner was relatively empty. I bit into a huge wedge of date and walnut loaf, wondering vaguely how Eva would manage during my two years' training at Queen's College for the ministry.

Poor Eva. It wasn't the first time she'd been left alone to bring up the children, and even when I was at home I always seemed to be involved in work or pursuing my own interests. Right now wasn't the best of times to be living away from home, either. Rae was at a crucial time in her education, which was one of the reasons we hadn't all packed our bags and moved to the Midlands and Iain was at that adolescent age where, if he was anything like his old man, he needed a father's firm hand. I pushed a few ominous thoughts to the back of my mind. No sense in looking for problems. Eva would cope. Eva always managed to cope. She had to, because for one reason or another I was never there. I pushed those guilty thoughts firmly to the back of my mind as well. No sense carrying a guilt complex around with me. The only way to resolve it was to ensure that when I qualified as a minister, I'd be less of a workaholic and spend more time with my family.

Meanwhile, if my studies permitted, I'd be able to return home most weekends because I still had the car. When I'd handed in my notice to the local authority I'd expected I'd have to sell my car since I'd bought it with a loan through the council. I prayed heart-rendingly over this issue. As far as I was concerned my car was an essential as there was no way I could afford to meet the cost of public transport to get me home at weekends. Then, a few days before I left for college, the local authority informed me that as long as I kept up the payments I could keep the car. That was just one of many solutions that fell neatly into place.

Over those final few weeks before starting college I grew more and more amazed by the way God met all our needs, especially our financial commitments. One morning, when I collected the post on the way to the breakfast table, I opened an envelope to find œ25 inside. It was the first of many gifts we received to help our finances over the next two years at college.

I poured hot, steaming tea into the cup of my thermos flask and sipped, worrying not for the first time how I would manage the studies. Now nearing my mid-forties I found studying increasingly difficult. It had not been one of my greatest assets in the first place and the awful memory always hovered of how I'd failed miserably last time I'd studied for the ministry, but this time I hoped I'd learned enough to know that God expected me to do my fair share of the work as well.

The interview had been very difficult for me. I shuddered when I remembered the influential bodies of ministers, psychologists and lay members of the Church who made up the board assembled for our two-day interview. The heavy, intensive atmosphere had me terrified and for the first time I realised how Robert and some of my lads must have felt under the scrutiny of the judge and court officials. Even so I didn't feel I'd done too badly until one of them starting asking awkward questions about my social work. I could feel myself becoming agitated by her tenacity. It was only with a great deal of effort that I managed to remain calm and polite.

The following morning I made my way into the dining room, anxiously wondering what sort of impression I'd made the day before. The principal of the College joined

174

our table for breakfast and was chatting amiably to those of us assembled for our second day of interviews.

'Nerve-racking experience these interviews, don't you think?' he said, turning to me.

'You're Alex Annand, aren't you?'

'Yes.'

'Good. I hoped to have a word with you.'

'Oh?' Having one's blood pressure raised over breakfast isn't the best of ways to start the day. The other two prospective students left the table, leaving us alone.

'You've travelled from Newcastle upon Tyne, haven't you?'

'Yes.'

'Social worker, aren't you?'

'I am.'

'Mmm. May I?' He poured himself a cup of tea from my pot. 'One of my students comes from the same background as you,' he said. 'We were talking earlier about the number of Methodist ministers who leave the church to go into social work. It's nice to see a reversal of roles.' He hesitated. 'Mind you, this chap nearly wasn't accepted because he was reluctant to talk about his calling. Fortunately in his final interview he managed to make it clear that this wasn't just a career move, but that God was indeed calling him into the ministry. It was a near thing, though.' He looked directly at me when he said, 'I noticed you didn't say too much about your calling when we interviewed you earlier.'

'Oh . . . well . . .'

'Anyway, you've got a second interview today. Perhaps we'll hear more about it then.' He looked at his watch. 'Better go. Nice to meet you, Mr Annand.'

'Yes, er . . . yes. Goodbye.'

175

After he'd left I sat thoughtfully pondering over what he'd said. Talking about my calling into the church was easier said than done. During my time with Peter and Jonathan, I'd thought of little else but my calling into the ministry of the Anglican Church and proudly told my friends, family and people I'd worked with of my intentions. So when I'd failed my exams and was rejected the embarrassment of having to say I'd made a mistake and that perhaps God wasn't calling me into the ministry after all was extremely humiliating. This time I'd made a point of keeping my big mouth shut. I wouldn't be made a fool of a second time.

I spent a good part of the morning wandering around the gardens and lawns, struggling to come to terms with the simple phrase, 'God has called me into the ministry', but although I knew he had, actually making that statement public was quite another matter.

'Why is it so difficult? Why?' As I thought and prayed carefully about this I concluded that I was still scarred by the humiliation, rejection and confusion caused by radical Christians. My time in Alnmouth with those gentle, quiet Franciscan friars had brought some healing in that it had restored a more balanced view of God and broadened my understanding of Christians but now, it seemed, I was having to face the very core of my pain. I was having to accept that Peter and Jonathan had been right all along. I was called into the ministry, and to say it out loud was in essence forgiving them and accepting that initial calling from God all those years ago.

'You've got me this far, Father,' I prayed. 'So I'll do anything, anything if you give me the courage to tell the whole story regarding my calling and get me into college. Father, God, if you do this for me I'll . . . I'll . . . even give up smoking!'

That afternoon I walked in to face the committee who were authorised to assess and test my calling. Questions came from all angles but today nothing seemed to agitate me, nothing distressed me. I even found myself relating the story of Peter and Jonathan and my calling, my failure, humiliations and disappointments and then the call again, twenty years later through Les while we were camping. In fact the final part I related with such humour and conviction that I surprised even myself.

Now here I was, at long last accepted as a student of Queen's College and on my way to Birmingham. I poured another cup of tea into the flask cup and sipped. The caffeine eased the niggling headache somewhat. Eva had warned me not to stay too long at the farewell do given by my colleagues at the local authority, but as usual I'd taken no notice.

'Dinna fret, Eva!' I rebuked jovially.

'You've a long journey on Sunday, Alex. You need to pack and spend some time with the children.'

'Aye, well, I'm not a drinking man, am I? So a couple of hours wi' ma colleagues'll do me no harm.'

A couple of hours had turned into a lively party with colleagues from Social Services and other departments as well. Despite the hilarity going on around me I found it a sad occasion. The strike, now over, had brought great changes. Colleagues who'd worked together for years in the once friendly local government department of Social Services no longer acknowledged each other. There were hurts and suspicions that would take time to heal and some that never would, but the fact that all these people had willingly put aside their differences and come together for my send-off was a step in the right direction and touched me deeply.

I put the top on my flask and reached into my pockets for a packet of cigarettes. 'Drat!' I looked at the empty packet in disgust. Stepping out of the car I made my way to the shop in the filling station. Suddenly I froze in my tracks.

'You made a contract.'

The memory of my prayer in the gardens of Queen's College when I'd rashly promised God that I would do anything, anything, even give up smoking, if he got me into college, flooded forcibly into my mind. For years I'd tried to give it up but become so irritable and bad-tempered that it was a relief to everyone around me when I started up again. I'd smoked since I was sixteen years of age, occasionally at first, but then, serving overseas in the army where cigarettes were cheap, it had turned into an unbreakable habit. Later, when I'd been working antisocial hours on the taxi rank, it had become a companion and when I moved into social work, a relief from stress.

'You made a contract.'

I stood undecided in the middle of the car park, craving a cigarette. A car skirted around me, its occupants peering curiously in my direction. I took a deep breath. 'Lord, I want to give up smoking. I'm willing to give up smoking, but quite simply I can't!'

Suddenly I remembered the advice Revd Gunn had given me about my swearing. 'If you've tried your best and failed, then hand it over to God. He will do the rest.' Slowly and deliberately I squashed the empty cigarette packet in my hand and threw it into a nearby bin, then turning abruptly on my heel I headed back towards the car. It was only as I started up the engine that I realised the craving for a cigarette had vanished. It never returned.

Other than a few initial hiccups, college turned out quite well. At the end of the first week all the students were allocated to groups led by one of the tutors. I'd experienced group therapy before in my social work studies and it wasn't something I enjoyed. In fact I hated it! On the first evening of our group meeting, I arrived early and was welcomed by the occupant of the flat, a fellow student now in his second year.

'You'll be expected to attend every Friday evening,' he informed us when we'd all assembled.

'I'm afraid I won't be able to come every Friday evening,' I apologised hesitantly.

'Really? Something better to do, have you?'

I didn't like his tone. In fact I'm ashamed to say I didn't like him very much either.

'Yes,' I replied smoothly. 'I intend to go home to see my wife and family some weekends.'

He gave a half-smile. 'You'll have to forget that! Life at college takes priority now.'

I'd come across this attitude before. It didn't bring out the best in me. I might have stopped smoking and even my swearing was almost non-existent now but my temper, although much improved, still left a lot to be desired. I got to my feet. 'That's tough!' I said, more loudly than I'd intended. 'Because I have every intention of going home to see my family and giving them priority in my life. In fact – I'm going now! Goodnight!' With that I marched out of the door, threw a few clothes into my suitcase, jumped in the car and sped up the motorway to see Eva and my children. On my return to college on Monday morning my tutor asked to see me. He wanted to discuss the minor upset in the group. He was very sympathetic and although he didn't approve of my outburst, he reassured me that I would indeed have time to spend some weekends at home.

The first few months at Queen's College found me so worried about failing exams again that I was continually studying.

'Relax a bit more, Alex. Get out and do something other than study and rush home at weekends,' my tutor advised me. Sound advice, but there wasn't anything I wanted to do – until I met Bessie. Bessie came in the shape of a large, green and rusty petrol-driven lawnmower and it was love at first sight. She and I became a standing joke around college: 'If you're looking for Alex, listen for the insidious roar of a lawnmower accompanied by Alex's whistle.' I discovered that the physically demanding task of mowing lawns was an ideal way to relax and clarify my thoughts for the work set before us, and because there was a lot of work the lawns were never lovelier than when I was a student at Queen's!

Reggie, one of the students I'd made friends with, popped his head round the door of my room one evening. Did you get an invitation to the special service for healing from the local church, Alex?'

I looked up from my book. 'What?'

'Church, Alex. God's house. Remember him?' Reggie raised his eyebrows mockingly.

'Aye, oh aye, the healing service, I'd forgotten all about that. Yes, I'll come. I think I'm brain-dead anyway.'

'Hurry up then. We've only ten minutes to get there and my car isn't to be relied on for starting first time.' He disappeared back to his own room down the corridor and I stretched, throwing my pencil on the bed. Yes, I needed a break from studying.

'Ready, Alex?' Reggie thumped on the door.

'Coming!' I grabbed my jacket and a few minutes later we were chugging along in his Beetle to a nearby church. The service was entitled 'Christian Healing' and was relevant to the area I was studying at the time, hence my decision to accept Reggie's invitation.

It began with a lively time of worship. I'd been to similar services led by evangelicals or charismatics in my home church and although that flavour of worship didn't do an awful lot for me, I mostly enjoyed it. Then came the moment when the minister called for all those who needed prayer for healing to come forward. While the organ played softly in the background, the first brave soul made a move from his seat and took the long walk to the front where the minister and his ministry team laid their hands upon him. To my absolute horror he suddenly toppled backwards. Fortunately one of the team members was standing behind him and caught him. I waited, expecting someone to rush to his aid, but no one seemed unduly worried that a member of their congregation was lying flat on his back on the floor in the middle of a service. In fact as various members of the congregation moved forward for prayer they just stepped over him. He wasn't the only one to fall either. At least half a dozen of them collapsed on the floor after having been prayed with. I discovered later that this was referred to as 'resting in the Spirit'.

I shuffled uneasily. I didn't care much for this! I glanced at Reggie sitting next to me. He appeared quite unperturbed by what was taking place. Was this phenomenon of God? If so it was all new to me and I didn't know what to make of it.

The well-dressed gentleman sitting next to me must have sensed my unease. He leant forward. 'Is this disturbing you?' he whispered.

I nodded. I knew he was the husband of one of the church stewards. He was also an ENT consultant in Birmingham. I'd met him on previous occasions when we'd visited the church.

'What's your opinion?' I whispered back.

He was quiet for a moment, then he said, 'The only thing that bothers me is, the people who've gone out there with terminal illnesses may come back tomorrow claiming to have been healed and sadly I will have to be the one to tell them they still have their cancers.' He hesitated before adding, 'I'm not denying that the healing power of God does exist and there are occasions when healing takes place. I just wish those in leadership would be a bit more careful when they say, "You've been healed" because in my experience it doesn't always work like that and people are given false hope.'

Hearing someone else voice their concerns, even though they weren't the same as mine, I found somewhat comforting. Unusually quiet and somewhat thoughtful, I made my way back to college with Reggie. I couldn't explain what had happened to disturb me but one thing was for sure: I wouldn't ever be involved in such a service or ministry as that!

‪₡ℜ‬ **20** ‪ℰᴑ‬

'You must be joking! No way! I'm not going back there!'

I don't think that was quite the right attitude to take to the post I was being offered. 'I'm not going back there!' I repeated stubbornly. The hurts, bitter experiences and near nervous breakdown I'd suffered as a social worker in that area swam painfully to the forefront of my mind. Unfortunately, as a probationer, that was no reason for me to refuse what was to be my first appointment as a Methodist minister and I had to get used to the idea.

A few days before we moved in, Eva and I took one of our rare days off together. It was a beautiful, clear summer's afternoon so we made our way up into the hills and found ourselves in a spot with a panoramic view of the bridges spanning the River Tyne. The spire of St Nicholas' Cathedral, where I'd given my life to Jesus, strained to reach the other tall buildings of the city, while across the river, cranes and scaffolding dominated the growing town of Gateshead. Both sides of the bridges were packed with places, people and experiences, good and bad. It was hard to believe I'd actually wanted to leave all this to return to my beloved Aberdeen. As I scanned the landscape, trying to identify buildings I recognised, my eyes fell upon the first of the three churches in my care. Although I'd come to terms with the fact that I had to accept this appointment and was actually quite excited about it, I couldn't seem to get rid of the awful memories that the place invoked, or the aggression, false accusations, stress and fear. I shuddered, despite the warm afternoon.

A few days later, while Eva saw to the removal men in the house, I wandered down to meet the church steward to have a look at one of my church halls which I'd been led to believe needed some work done to it. I'd been led to believe correctly! My heart sank fast as I surveyed the faded brown picture of John Wesley concealing a large damp patch on the wall. Other pictures, I discovered, were strategically placed for exactly the same reason. The paintwork was flaking and there were also a few broken windows.

'But it's the dry rot that's the problem,' the church steward informed me.

'Dry rot?'

'Aye, and it's worse than we thought.' He saw me looking at the broken windows. 'The hooligans hereabouts kicked them in but the trouble came when the builders came to mend them. They bricked around the glass but they also bricked around the existing wooden frames as well and when we came to decorate we found . . .' he glanced at me apprehensively.

'Dry rot,' I finished the sentence for him. 'So for all you know it could be all over.' I waved my arm in the general direction of the rafters and floorboards.

He nodded. 'Not to worry, Mr Annand. We'll raise the money somehow.'

'Aye,' I said, in a tone that didn't indicate any confidence in his remark. 'Well, thanks for the tour of inspection, Mr Jackson. It's been enlightening if nothing else.'

I made my way back to the manse in a none too happy frame of mind. Here I was in my mid-forties, a minister of the Church of God, full of enthusiasm to preach the Gospel and fulfil my calling and what had I been faced with? Dry rot! None of my training had prepared me to cope with dampness, crumbling church halls, money raising or any of the other skills that would be needed to cope with the three ageing church buildings now in my care.

I opened the door of my new home and walked straight into a china cabinet. 'What the . . . Eva! What's the china cabinet doing in the middle of the hall? Why didn't the removal men put it where you wanted it?' I squeezed past it, climbed over a sofa and literally fell into the living room where Rae and Iain sat watching television on a couple of packing-cases.

'Aye. That's right!' I said angrily. 'Let's get our priorities sorted. Television first then . . .'

'Don't start, Alex,' Eva warned.

'Don't start! I've just walked into a blasted china cabinet! Hang on! We haven't got a china cabinet! What's going on?'

'Didn't Bob Jackson tell you?'

'Not exactly. We got a bit bogged down with dry rot in the church hall. Tell me what?'

Eva ran her fingers wearily through her hair. 'It belongs to the previous minister. The removal men could only get half their furniture into their van. Back in a few days, they said, but I don't know how I'm going to fit all their stuff and ours into this house, even for a few days!' She gestured helplessly at the overcrowded living room and hall. I caught her hand in mid-flight and squeezed it reassuringly. 'Dinna worry, Eva. It'll all work out.'

'I seem to have heard that phrase before,' she remarked dryly.

'I'll give Bob Jackson a ring after dinner. That is if I've got any dinner?'

'You have. Put your coat on again. It'll take you two minutes to get to the fish and chip shop!'

That night we ate off packing-cases and slept in bedrooms piled high with furniture. The following morning we'd hardly had time to finish breakfast before there was a knock on the door. Rae shrieked and fled upstairs. In her new role as minister's daughter she wouldn't be seen dead with her hair in curlers, and Eva shot into the kitchen in her dressing-gown. Iain raised his eyebrows questioningly

185

before returning to the settee in front of the television with his cornflakes. I sighed and went to answer the door.

Bob Jackson stood on the doorstep with half a dozen heavyweights behind him. 'Hello, Revd Annand. I know it's early but after your telephone call last night I thought we ought to rally round and see if we can't find somewhere else for the furniture left by your predecessor. Help you settle in, so to speak.' He beamed at me like an oversized cherub.

I was about to say thank you and plan an action campaign, when a huge bloke with torn jeans and a lurid picture on his T-shirt stepped forward. 'I'm Barry, vicar. Just say the word. We'll sort y' out!'

I had no doubt he would. Visions of the previous sortings out I'd had in the army came vividly to mind.

'Thank you,' I began, when a figure built like a sumo wrestler rolled up behind Barry. 'Sort y'out,' he grunted.

Fortunately Bob Jackson intervened. 'Start with the stuff in the front room, lads,' he ordered.

'Front room!' grunted the sumo wrestler, shoulder-charging me out of the way as he followed Barry through the front door.

'Some of the ladies will be down this afternoon to help clean,' Bob said, peering over my shoulder at the shambles behind me. 'They've been baking pies and the like.'

I heard Eva's footstep behind me as she joined me at the door. 'That's very kind of you, Mr Jackson, but there's no need for you to go to all that trouble. Really.'

'No trouble, dear lady. No trouble at all, and the name's Bob.'

'Mind y' back, Bob.' Barry and the sumo wrestler butted me out of the way carrying a brightly coloured settee. I was relieved to see that Iain and his cornflakes weren't still on it.

'The ladies will be pleased to meet you, Mrs Annand.'

'Eva. Call me Eva.'

A couple more lads pushed past us with packing-cases and Barry and the sumo wrestler returned to the house via the neat display of marigolds around the borders of the front lawn. They emerged a few minutes later with the china cabinet.

For the rest of that day the manse and garden swarmed with men and women willing to help us to settle into our new home. It was only towards the end of the day that I realised the warm glow inside me was due more to the kindness of these good folk than the ladies' home-made pies.

A few weeks later I was in my overalls, quite alone in the church hall at the top of a pair of suspiciously unstable ladders.

'So this is your introduction to the ministry, Alex,' I muttered. A lump of plaster fell on my head. 'You're not preaching the glorious word of God or ministering to his flock, you're grovelling in muck and dust.' Of course I didn't need to be part of the labouring team to deal with the dry rot. It wasn't expected of me but I was always one to get thoroughly involved and Bob, Barry, the sumo wrestler and a few others had worked solidly all day Saturday while I'd prepared Sunday's sermon. Now today, Monday, I decided to do my bit. I pulled more plaster down and a few grains trickled down my back. I was getting dirtier by the minute when the silence of the hall was suddenly shattered by a voice behind me. 'Hoy, mate!'

I jumped and the ladders shook precariously. 'Yes?'

A workman in a pair of dirty blue overalls and faded cap stood at the hall door.

'Where's that **** Sandy? He wants me to move these **** chairs from the **** hall to the **** kitchen. What the **** he wants to do that for beats me. Have you **** seen 'im, mate?'

I shook the plaster from my hair and turned to face the blasphemer. 'I don't know nowt about that, mate,' I said. 'I'm just the minister!'

There was an ominous silence while the contours of his face changed momentarily, then he grinned. 'Well, you should **** dress like a **** minister!'

His language was real rough-and-ready stuff. Nothing new to me. I'd heard it all before. I'd used it all before, too, so I wasn't shocked by it and I think my acceptance of him and these kind, down-to-earth folk in my church and community, not only won me their hearts but also brought their own brand of acceptance, love and healing into mine.

Not that they were all ministering angels by any stretch of the imagination. From time to time they gave me my fair share of headaches. Not least at the Church Council meetings! Although I had chaired meetings and sat on various committees throughout my adult life, nothing, but nothing had prepared me for the Church Council meeting.

188

This, I reflected as I sat through a stormy one, was not Christianity at its best!

It was a kind of free-for-all, with sharp words and criticisms flying to and fro. Aware of my responsibility to care not only for the church buildings but for the people, I was determined to do my job properly and try to put a stop to such goings-on. I soon learned to become very suspicious of the phrase 'I'm telling you this in Christian love,' because in my experience it became another way of saying, 'You're not going to like what I'm about to say but I'm going to say it anyway!' Their openness and freshness was a bit too open and fresh for my liking.

'Divind fret yerself, minister! Once it's said it's soon forgotten!' I was consoled. I remained unconvinced and some evenings went home and spent a sleepless night, I was so upset by their frankness. This surely wasn't the way Christian folk should speak to one another? In time Eva was persuaded to join the Church Council but after one such disastrous meeting she arrived home and said, 'Well, that's it! Never again! I'm resigning!' And she did! But gradually, during the next four years, Church Council meetings did improve and my confidence in chairing them grew enormously.

I learned much from these outspoken but kind and generous folk and received far more than I gave. I found myself whistling cheerfully as I physically worked alongside the men and women of the church in their overalls, pulling down ceilings, chipping plaster off walls, painting and decorating. I became a mine of information on dry rot, woodwork and dampness, and a genius at finding ways to raise money for church funds.

My appointment as chaplain to the mayor brought me unexpectedly into contact with my former employers in Social Services, some of whom had caused me much pain. I expected to feel uncomfortable, bitter, have a few sleepless nights churning over past experiences even, but was surprised to discover that nothing like that happened.

Some sort of healing had been taking place inside me. I likened it to the way we'd mended my church hall with its dry rot, dampness and rotten floorboards. In the same way I was slowly being mended and restored through the Christian love of my flock. Being accepted by them built up my confidence in the community so that gradually I found I was able to look at those experiences in my past with a different perspective.

'Revd Glover's been on the telephone,' Eva informed me as I walked through the door one evening. 'Something about inviting you to be hospital chaplain.'

'What? Not likely! Couldn't fancy that! I've had enough of hospitals to last me a lifetime! I hope you told him no, definitely not!'

Two weeks later I look up the post of hospital chaplain.

'I hate hospitals,' I complained to Eva. 'They're full of sick people.'

After three months comments from various quarters filtered through about my work: 'Mind, when he comes to visit in hospital he doesn't stay long.' 'He's straight in and straight out. Doesn't hang around.'

I was hurt and disturbed by these criticisms but after thinking deeply about what they'd said, I had to admit there was a certain amount of truth in them. Although I enjoyed my work as a minister I wasn't so keen about this new role as hospital chaplain, and I never stayed very long at people's bedsides unless it was absolutely necessary. Eventually it dawned on me that once again the problem lay with my own painful memories of childhood sickness and the times I'd had to spend in hospital. Slowly but surely it seemed that God was healing disturbing memories from my past. Perhaps it was time for him and me to sort this one out as well.

Those years of my first appointment passed swiftly. During that time I had been ordained, seen the congregation grow, eradicated the dry rot and come to love the people deeply.

After five years, however, I knew that the time had come for me to move on, although I was sad to leave. But when I obtained an appointment in Sunderland, I began to get excited about the new opportunities that lay before me.

On our arrival at our new home, I learned that the husband of one of the church stewards was to go into hospital, possibly for major heart surgery. Eva looked horrified when at 8.00am I announced I was going to visit them. 'You can't call on folk at such an early hour, especially on a Sunday morning,' she rebuked.

'Yes, I can. They're members of my church,' I retorted obstinately, pulling on my jacket.

They lived about half a mile away. As I knocked on the door I noticed the curtains were still drawn and uneasily it dawned on me that Eva probably had a point. It was a rather early hour of the morning to be calling on anyone. A startled lady, hugging a pink flowered dressing-gown around her and struggling to cover a rainbow assortment of curlers held in a hairnet, answered the door. Her mouth fell open when she saw who it was.

'Oh, minister! Oh dear! I'm afraid you've caught me!'

I cut through her embarrassment. 'Dinna fret yourself, Mrs Evans. I just thought I'd come and have a word with you and your husband before he goes into hospital today.' 'That's very kind of you, Mr Annand.'

I followed her upstairs where her husband was having his early morning cup of tea. I discovered him to be a talkative chap and, although surprised to receive the minister at such an unearthly hour, he nevertheless welcomed my visit. We talked for a while and in the course of the conversation he told me how, ever since he'd been a kid, he'd wanted to be a bus driver. Then only a few weeks ago his childhood ambition had been fulfilled when the local bus company had employed him. The only trouble was, if his heart condition turned out to be serious, he'd lose his job. He was obviously very concerned and almost in tears when he came to the end of his story.

'Would you like me to pray with you?' I asked. He nodded his head. I stood up and for some inexplicable reason I had a strong desire to place my hands on his head. 'Don't be stupid, Alex!' I rebuked myself silently. 'You've never done that sort of thing before. A simple prayer is all that's needed.' But as I moved forward to the bedside I knew I couldn't ignore this prompting. Standing awkwardly by his bed, I gently laid my hands upon his head, praying for God to bring him healing and peace. Then, concluding the prayer, I left the house wondering what on earth had got into me! Perhaps I should have taken Eva's advice and stayed at home. Early morning fresh air had a peculiar effect on me.

It was over two weeks before I saw Mrs Evans again and even then I didn't recognise her.

'Mr Annand! Yoo-hoo! Mr Annand!' She bustled up to me as I was leaving the church at the end of the evening service.

'I've been trying to catch you for the last week, Mr Annand,' she said breathlessly. 'But every time I've telephoned you've been out.'

'Oh?' I frantically tried to place where I'd seen her face before.

She smiled and with typical feminine insight recognised my dilemma. 'I'm Mrs Evans. One of your church stewards?' she gently prompted me. 'You came and prayed with my husband very early one Sunday morning before he was taken into hospital.'

The penny dropped. 'Oh, yes! Didn't recognise you with your clothes on . . . I mean dressed, with your hair . . . er. How is he?'

She chuckled. 'He's wonderful, Mr Annand. Wonderful. And the most amazing thing happened. When they got him to the hospital they couldn't find a thing wrong with him. They kept him in for the rest of the week doing all sorts of tests on him, then they let him out wondering why he'd been sent to them in the first place. It's amazing. When you prayed like that, laying hands on him and all, I never dreamt he would get better so soon. You've got a real healing gift there, Mr Annand. There's real power in those hands of yours.'

I stared at her, horrified. 'Now don't start that nonsense! If your husband is better it's nowt to do with me. God is the one who's taken care of him. Anyway, are you sure the hospital have finished their tests?'

'Absolutely!'

'Aye, well do me a favour and don't go around telling folk I've got healing hands. That sort of talk only leads to trouble.'

'Oh?'

'Aye. For a start it might stir up hope in people that I certainly can't fulfil!'

I returned home aware of an uncomfortable gnawing in the pit of my stomach. I remembered the healing service I'd attended when I'd been at college. According to the consultant sitting next to me, when people had flaked out on the floor many had believed, or been led to believe, that healing had taken place, only to discover that their illness was still with them when they went to the hospital. Healing was a very controversial and dangerous thing to play around with.

I continued to puzzle over Jack Evans and was, to say the least, quite disturbed by the whole episode. However, I was more than delighted to see him back at church and even more delighted when he was officially given a clean bill of health and fulfilled his lifelong ambition, driving his double-decker bus.

Healing? No, Lord! I can't cope with that! Not healing!

☙ 21 ❧

A short time after this incident with the Evanses, I was asked to visit Lillie, an elderly Christian lady who was dying of cancer. She was extremely distressed and confided that she was frightened of dying. I reminded and assured her that there was a God who loved her, and that she was promised a place in his kingdom. She listened. We talked for a while, then I held her frail, wrinkled hands in mine and said a short prayer, asking God to give her peace and reassurance.

I visited her regularly and soon became aware of a gradual deterioration in her condition. One day I received a telephone call from one of her nieces. 'Revd Annand? Joyce Norman here. It's my aunt. I'm afraid she hasn't got long to go. I wonder if you'd mind calling to see her again? She's been asking for you.'

'No problem,' I assured her. 'I can come this afternoon. Will that be all right?' I found her nieces sitting solemnly in the kitchen having a cup of tea when I arrived. 'Just go straight up, Mr Annand,' Joyce said. 'You know the way.'

I found Lillie lying back on her pillows, frail, white and extremely agitated. I sat on the bed beside her, took her small, bony hand in mine and, under the assumption that she was worrying about dying again, quietly talked to her about it. After a while I laid my hand on her brow and as I quietly prayed she seemed to calm down. She closed her eyes and when I saw her breathing become more even, I crept out of the bedroom.

'She's sleeping peacefully,' I informed her nieces as I hurried through the kitchen on my way to my next appointment.

I was exhausted when I got home at the end of the day and flopped into the armchair, kicking off my shoes.

'I'd put those back on again if I were you,' Eva greeted me. 'Urgent telephone call from Joyce Norman. Can you go round to the house immediately?'

'I've just been!'

'I know, but they want you back.'

I returned to the house expecting to hear that Auntie had died but when I knocked at the door I was surprised to be met by two very excited nieces.

'What have you done to Auntie?' Joyce asked, beaming all over her face.

'What do you mean?'

'She's sleeping like a baby.'

I followed them into the kitchen, puzzled. 'Well, that's good, isn't it? She's been getting herself all worked up worrying about dying.'

Joyce steered me towards the kitchen chair while her sister poured me a cup of tea.

'Mr Annand,' she said quietly, 'Auntie won't get any better. She's dying, we all know that. The cancer has spread throughout her whole body. The doctors warned us that once it reached her head she would suffer terribly and never be free of pain. In the last few weeks we've watched her suffer more and more from excruciating headaches, and the doctors can do very little to help her except give her more painkillers.' She shook her head and her eyes were full of tears. 'She's hardly slept for days but, Mr Annand, whatever you did, my aunt has slept peacefully since you left and when she woke up she . . . she had no pain in her head. None at all!'

I stared at her in disbelief. 'Surely you're not trying to tell me she's cured of cancer? She's too far gone for that!'

'No, I'm not saying that. I'm simply telling you that the terrible pain my aunt had in her head has gone. God answered your prayers, Mr Annand. He's taken away her pain.'

Two weeks later Lillie died and during that time she was at peace in her mind and her headaches never returned. Although I was pleased for Lillie and her nieces I remained uneasy. Questions about healing reverberated around my head and, try as I might to forget them, they wouldn't go away. One morning I decided to tackle my boss about it in my den over a cup of tea and a packet of chocolate digestive biscuits.

'Right, Lord! What's going on?' I sank down into my favourite faded chair which had lost its springs, put my feet on the desk and for once in my life made a determined effort to enter into a time of quietness before God.

As I contemplated this question of healing I began to realise how much of it I'd experienced in my own life. My mind wandered to the bitter memories I'd had of Peter and Jonathan and radical Christianity, where I'd been left feeling worthless, not up to scratch, unwanted by God and the Church. Yet God had brought healing to me through those gentle Franciscan friars who had drawn alongside me in friendship, so that my sense of worthlessness had faded and I'd been able to forgive and develop a love for all God's people. I recalled the stressful memories of my social work days and my apprehension at returning to that very area as a minister; the rough-and-ready folk I'd been brought into contact with had shown me so much love and kindness that I could honestly say there was no longer any resentment or desire for revenge. Then there was my work as hospital chaplain. There was no longer any need for me to rush away from the wards when I visited the sick. Those childhood memories were still vivid but no longer brought back the fears they used to.

I helped myself to another biscuit. God was healing my memories. Of that I was sure. I could also remember being physically pain-free after Peter and Emma and the missionaries had prayed to God to heal me. It seemed to me that God must love me an awful lot to be bothered to do all this for me. ME! Then the thought occurred to me that, as God had used others to bring his healing to me, he may want me to bring his healing and comfort to others. But how? Laying hands on the sick? Was that what had happened to Mr Evans and Lillie? Could a bloke like me, with all my faults and hang-ups, be used in such a way? How could God even consider me?

I ate another biscuit. So, I concluded, where was all this getting me? I believed in a God who could heal. I had to. But actually being involved in a ministry of healing was quite another matter. It wasn't something I'd contemplated when I entered the ministry and I still had deep reservations about the healing services I'd experienced so far . . . I suddenly realised I'd finished the packet of biscuits and guiltily stuffed the empty packet into the drawer of my desk to avoid Eva finding out. She reckoned I was putting on too much weight. I sighed, got to my feet and pulled on my shoes. I'd meditated long enough and hadn't really come to any conclusions! Meditating, at least my style of meditating, was extremely fattening!

The following Friday I visited one of the children from Sunday school who was having his tonsils out. He lay in the hospital bed with his face as white as the pillows and the sheets that covered him. The poor kid was obviously terrified.

'How's it going, Steve?' I bellowed in my usual loud voice as I walked the length of the children's ward towards him.

He turned big tearful eyes upon me as I reached his bedside. 'OK,' he whispered, 'but I'm a bit scared and lonely. I don't know anyone.'

I patted his hand reassuringly. 'Scared? Nowt to be scared about getting your tonsils out, son. I spent months and months in a hospital when I was your age.'

A tear trickled down his cheek. 'Oh?' he said, without interest. He obviously couldn't have cared less about my time in hospital.

'Aye,' I continued. 'And if you promise not to tell your mam I'll tell you about Sister Jackson and how I had to crawl under all the beds to escape from her ward.'

A spark of interest flared. 'Escape?'

'Aye. She was a dragon was Sister Jackson and I was much more poorly than you. You're just getting your tonsils out. I had . . . well, I was very ill and could hardly walk. But my mate Ben dared me to get out of the ward and find out what was in the room at the end of the corridor, so . . .' I saw I'd got his attention so set about embellishing the story. I was just getting to the exciting part when I realised that half the children in the ward were sitting around the bed, transfixed.

' . . . so I slowly turned the handle of the forbidden room. The door creaked and . . . and . . . ' I stopped suddenly at the sight of Matron pounding down the ward towards us. ' . . . and I'll tell you what happened when I visit Steve tomorrow. After he's had his tonsils out. Do you think you'll remember where I left off?'

There were choruses of 'Yes!' Yes!' as I left a much more cheerful and popular Steve. 'I always know when you visit, Mr Annand, by the noise in the ward,' Matron remarked dryly as I passed her, but I think there was a twinkle in her eye and a smile around her lips.

The following day I had two funerals to conduct, a sermon to write and a ladies' meeting to speak at so time was of the utmost importance, but having promised Steve I'd return I hurried along to the hospital. I found him playing on the floor with a few of the other children.

'Hello,' he said. 'What are you doing here?'

I was a bit taken aback. 'I promised to come back and see you to finish the story.'

198

He grinned. 'Any chance of you finishing it at Sunday school, Mr Annand? I'm a bit busy at the moment playing with my new friends. Thanks for calling, though.' He gave me an almost dismissive wave.

'Oh God!' I thought. 'And I've had such a busy day.'

I gave him and the other children a cheery wave as I hurried out of the ward, but heart-rending sobbing from one of the cubicles stopped me dead in my tracks. I popped my head around the curtain. A little girl of about two or three in pink rabbit pyjamas and with brown curly hair was wrapped in her mother's arms, crying profusely. The young mother looked pale and exhausted.

'Och! We canna have your bairn crying like this, can we?' I said. 'I'm Revd Alex Annand. Hospital chaplain.' I went over to where the mother sat and placed my hand gently on the child's head. 'There, there, lass. The peace of the Lord be with you. Hush your crying now. There, there.' I gently stroked her hot forehead and the child lifted red-rimmed eyes towards me in surprise. I stood for a while beside the young mother until, after a few more deep sobs, the child nestled up to her, closed her eyes and a few minutes later fell into a deep sleep.

The mother looked up at me and her own eyes filled with tears as she smiled. 'She's cried and cried all day. You're the only one that's been able to quieten her. I can't believe it.'

Little did she know that neither could I! 'Aye, well, some of us have got it and others haven't. Ta-ta, pet!' I made a hasty retreat.

'It's nice to see you can bring some peace and quiet to the ward as well as noise,' Matron remarked as I passed her office. 'That child has been crying all day. None of us have been able to settle her.'

'Coincidence!' I told myself as I hurried out of the hospital. 'Don't start looking for things that aren't there, Alex.'

199

It was a month later. I was standing at the door of the church saying goodnight to the congregation when a young lady came up to me. I'd noticed her sitting at the back of the church while I'd been preaching.

'I know you're not one of my regulars at church,' I said, 'But I vaguely recognise your face.'

She smiled. 'I'm Shirley's mum.'

'Shirley?' I racked my brains to bring any Shirleys I might know to mind. None came.

'You prayed for my daughter in the hospital.'

The light dawned. 'The little girl in the rabbit pyjamas sobbing her heart out! How is she?'

'She's fine now. You don't know what you did, Mr Annand.'

'Me? I didn't do anything.'

'Yes, you did. My child had been crying like that for over twenty-four hours and neither doctors, nurses nor medication could calm her down. Then you came in, said your little prayer and she slept for over twelve hours. The doctors were so pleased with her quick recovery she was allowed home much sooner than we expected.'

'That's grand to hear.' I shook her hand, jovially wished her goodnight then joked on with the rest of the congregation as they left the church in an attempt to hide my acute embarrassment.

I walked home, firmly pushing the incident to the back of my mind, or trying to. Healing! The word would not go away. The need people had for healing would not go away, either. Late though it was I made a pot of tea and took a packet of chocolate digestive biscuits through into my den. I turned on the bar of the electric fire, pulled off my shoes, sank into my comfortable chair and put my feet on the desk. I was all set for another meditation.

'What's going on, Lord?'

I didn't really need to ask. For the past couple of weeks, the idea of holding a healing service had been running around my head.

'That's a crazy idea,' I informed God. 'I've too many unanswered questions about healing myself to consider holding healing services.' I dived into the chocolate digestive biscuits. 'For instance, why do you heal some people and not others? Why do you sometimes heal non-believers instead of Christians, which you do if some of the books I've read are to be believed? How would I answer the questions of those who feel they're not good enough to be healed? In fact, how can I answer anybody's questions?' For more than an hour my mind whirled around with questions for which he didn't appear to give me any answers.

'OK, Lord! Just supposing it is your will and not an idea of my own that I start healing services in the church? Where do I go from here? You'll have to make it clear. You know I'm never still long enough to listen! In fact, why can't you speak to me now?'

I suddenly realised the teapot was empty, the biscuits were finished and it was well after midnight. He was probably telling me to get myself to bed. Stuffing the empty packet in the drawer I wearily made my way upstairs.

My first step of action was to speak to two colleagues who were already involved in the healing ministry. I shared with them my recent experiences and thoughts and in return they encouraged me with my vague ideas for holding healing services. Their advice and encouragement proved invaluable. The second thing I did was to call a church meeting, a very Methodist thing to do, to talk about the possibility of starting a service in one of my three churches especially for people who wanted prayer for healing. To my surprise over forty people turned up.

I'd read only a little about healing so was shamefully quite ignorant about the subject and my experiences had been confusing and spasmodic, so good sound teaching and guidance were missing and I had no clear idea of what we should be aiming for. However, much to my amazement, by the end of the evening our first healing service had been planned. I walked home in a daze, stunned by the speed with which the service had been planned and the enthusiasm of the people involved. I had expected to do much more research and reading about the subject but it seemed that events were moving quicker than my studies. 'I've heard of stepping out in faith, Lord, but I've really got the jitters over this one!'

Three weeks later the team, made up of volunteers from our meeting, met for prayer in the vestry before the service. To say I was nervous was the understatement of the year. I was like a cat on hot bricks. The prayer time did nothing for my fraught nerves, although the rest of the team seemed uplifted by it. Twice I crept out of the prayer meeting on some pretext or other to see how many folk had turned up. Finally our prayer meeting drew to a close, we anointed one another with oil and the team prepared to take up their various posts of stewards, readers, tea-makers and so on. I was left standing in the vestry with Herbert Witherington, one of our local preachers. 'I think I'll just check to see how many folk have arrived,' I said, making for the door. 'You've been checking every ten minutes since you arrived, Alex,' Herbert remonstrated. 'Don't worry. It'll be fine.'

'Aye, well, there were only about twenty people last time I looked.'

Herbert laughed. I'd taken a real liking to this quiet local preacher. He was a man in his mid-sixties whose sound advice and calming influence I'd grown to greatly appreciate, although neither were doing me much good at the moment. 'This is a big moment for many of us, Alex,' he said quietly.

'Oh?' I continued pacing the vestry floor. Next time it needed carpeting I'd know the measurements by heart.

'Long before you arrived our small prayer group had prayed for someone to lead us into this type of ministry of healing.'

'Lead you into . . . Herbert, I haven't a clue about healing!'

'Then it's a good job it's in the Lord's hands, Alex.'

'Oh God!' I paced across the floor diagonally this time. 'Do you think I should have a look to see how many . . .'

'No need. The Lord will send those he wants. Anyway, Ivy has just been through to say that two bus loads have arrived.'

'Two bus loads! Good Go . . . grief! Where from? Who told them?'

'Calm yourself, Alex. It's almost half-past. Are you ready?'

I shook my head. 'No, I'm not. Definitely not!' Nevertheless I adjusted my robes, composed myself and breathed a silent prayer. 'HELP!'

As I walked into the church and up to the pulpit with Herbert, a sea of faces greeted me. The church was packed. Over one hundred and sixty people had turned up. Where they had all come from I had no idea. The only thing I remember about the service was the wave of relief when it was all over. I was tense and nervous the whole time.

I know I began the service by explaining why we were all there. 'I don't have any healing powers of my own but I come here in faith. I come despite having questions and doubts but I come because I believe, as do the rest of the team, that this is where God wants us to be and we trust that his healing power is very much a part of what your doctor or the hospital does. God wants to bring healing and wholeness into lives that are sick . . .' I continued to reassure the congregation that this service was not about strange phenomena but about allowing the God of love and peace and healing to touch our lives. The moment came when I invited people to come forward for the laying on of hands by myself and two or three other members of the team. I didn't expect a great response so I was quite surprised when a trickle of people moved forward. A few minutes later the trickle became a flood as over fifty people responded to the call. I was amazed.

It was only as we were singing the last hymn that I glanced at my watch. 9.30pm! We'd been going two full hours! There'd be complaints. I'd get lynched! My desperate attempts to catch the eyes of the tea ladies to cancel tea proved useless. 'Two hours! We've been going for two whole hours!' I hissed to Herbert standing next to me.

He opened his eyes from prayer and patiently answered, 'Yes, Alex, and what a wonderful two hours!'

Over tea everyone spoke of the tremendous sense of peace they had felt during the service. One lady with a very severe health problem described it as something coming towards her like a gushing of rivers. She was never cured of her actual illness but over the months that followed she testified that she was able to live comfortably with it which previously she'd found too difficult to do. Others spoke of a deep awareness of the presence of God. I hadn't experienced a thing! But what I did notice that night was the expression of joy on so many faces.

To my surprise no one mentioned the time factor. At 10.30pm I had to say, 'Ladies and gentlemen. It has been wonderful having you, but would you please go home!'

It was only as these services of healing and wholeness developed and found a regular place in the life of our church and circuit that I began to relax and feel more at ease with the comfortable, unthreatening style that developed. We were very aware of the presence of God moving amongst us as we worshipped, and, as we came before him for healing, many experienced his healing power and peace in their lives. But I shall never forget my nervousness and fears of that first night.

'You preached magnificently, Alex,' Herbert enthused. 'You were absolutely glowing.'

'Oh, aye. That was me on fire with fear,' I retorted.

'You've certainly started something new and exciting in our circuit,' Herbert said. 'And added a new dimension to your own ministry.'

Yes, I suppose I had.

∞ 22 ∞

'We're happy to invite you to our circuit as superintendent minister,' said the voice at the other end of the telephone.

It seemed like only yesterday yet here I was in the second year of this appointment. It hadn't been easy saying goodbye to the Evanses, Joyce Norman and her sister, Herbert Witherington and the other friends we'd made, yet Eva and I had felt that the time was right to move on.

We discovered that the main and largest church in the circuit was thriving and growing. Sunday morning service in this village church meant pews packed with people of all ages. The other church in my care was situated some five miles away with a somewhat elderly congregation who were nevertheless keen and enthusiastic, with a renowned reputation for their hospitality and wonderful cream teas.

From day one, Eva and I were accepted warmly and felt very much at home. Then, some months after my arrival, I met with a group of folks who were eager to be involved in services of healing and wholeness. I was also privileged to be invited once again to be chaplain to the mayor of Gateshead.

Rae and Iain were grown. Rae was now married and we were blessed with a lovely grandson, Andrew. Eva took a part-time job in a craft shop, but what surprised me most was the way she had grown in confidence. She even accepted the role of president of the ladies' group as well as taking on other leadership roles. Now in my late fifties, I was a very happy, settled, contented man – until the day I went to visit Joan.

Joan and her husband were among the new friends we'd made in the village church. She was one of our local preachers and appeared to be a very level-headed sort of person, at least that's what I thought, until she began to recount with great enthusiasm the experience of her visit to the Sunderland Christian Centre, an Assemblies of God church.

'. . . and as I lay there on the floor I thought . . .' she paused for breath. She certainly needed to. She'd never shut up since I'd walked through her front door! '. . . I thought, I feel a bit like a squashed rag doll being refilled with stuffing again. I was exhausted but refreshed, if you know what I mean?'

I didn't, but I let her continue.

'But it was my legs.'

'Your legs?'

She nodded. 'Even after I sat up they refused to work. They were like jelly. Eventually I struggled to my feet. Around me people had fallen like flies. Some were shaking, others crying, some were even laughing.'

'Laughing?'

'Yes, you know, laughing.'

'Yes, I know what laughing is.' The more she told me the more uneasy I grew.

'But back to my legs.'

'Yes, let's not forget your legs.'

She gave me a withering glance. 'As the evening drew to a close, I struggled to my feet but my legs were so wobbly I didn't have the energy to step over all the dozens of bodies sprawled across the floor, so with a friend either side of me we had to zigzag around them.'

'Oh Lord!' I thought. What's she getting into?'

I sat patiently listening to Joan pouring out this incredible story, thinking, 'I knew this was going to be a difficult day. I just knew it!' I became even more concerned when she let slip that several members of our congregation had also been to this church. But whatever my reservations, I couldn't deny that something had happened to Joan. I was seeing a deep inner joy I'd never seen before.

She paused. 'So what do you think?'

I stumbled for an appropriate response. I didn't want to dampen her enthusiasm. 'I've seen people falling down before,' I said carefully.

'This is different. New,' she persisted. 'A couple of weeks ago I heard that their Pastor, Ken Gott, and his wife Lois had visited a church in Toronto. They returned full of enthusiastic reports of what God was doing there and within days the same phenomena were taking place in their Sunderland church.' Joan's face shone. 'I wish you could have been there, Alex.'

I didn't!

'In fact,' she continued, 'Why don't you come with me next time I go?'

'Well, I'm er . . . can't er . . . have to think about . . . er . . .' Thankfully I managed to avoid Joan's invitation and drove home puzzled and concerned. 'I hope this isn't going to be another of those situations that result in divisions within the church,' I thought apprehensively. 'I don't want any upset. Not now, Lord, not when things are going so well.'

For the next few days I couldn't seem to get Joan's extraordinary story out of my mind. I finally decided that I ought to go and see if this 'thing' was of God, especially if members of my congregations were going along. And so it was I found myself speeding down the motorway to Sunderland with Joan and Ann.

Ann and her family were also church members and I was very glad she'd agreed to come. She was an intelligent, quiet and discerning sort of person. She was a good counterbalance to Joan's enthusiastic nature and if Joan was going to do strange things at Sunderland I would be glad of Ann's reliable support. I kept up a cheerful banter from the back seat of Joan's car to hide my acute nervousness over the forthcoming evening. Why was I so nervous, I kept asking myself. Joan accelerated, moved into overdrive and shot past a convoy of lorries. No wonder I was nervous. If she continued driving like this I wouldn't have to worry about a visit to Sunderland. Meeting with Jesus would be a firsthand reality!

The new, spacious church hall, situated in the docklands of Sunderland, was built to hold six to seven hundred comfortably but half an hour before the service we found it almost full to capacity. I had already decided to go with as open a mind as possible, determined not to be critical of the style of worship I imagined I might find there. My first unease came when I recognised two people from one of my previous circuits and several more from my congregation.

'Hold it!' I drew back and under the pretext of fastening my shoelace, using Ann and Joan as a screen outside the gents' toilets until the two people disappeared into the crowd. For some strange reason it was important to me not to be recognised. I didn't want anyone interpreting my visit here to mean 'if the minister's here it must be all right'. I couldn't have that. I was only here to observe what was going on. In no way did I want to be identified with it! With difficulty we found three seats together towards the rear of the hall and waited for the service to begin.

If I had expected someone who could attract six hundred to a thousand people into his church, six nights a week, to be dynamic as well as charismatic, I was about to be disappointed, for the pastor and his wife, probably somewhere in their forties, appeared to be very ordinary people.

'He used to be in the police force,' Joan informed me.

I nodded. He looked like an ex-copper and I soon discovered he had the humour to go with it!

'Who's here for the first time? Ken's voice echoed through the mike. I firmly crossed my arms, whispering to Joan, 'I'm not letting on.'

'If you're here for the first time, curious perhaps as to what's going on, relax, and be open to whatever Jesus Christ has for you. This is a safe environment to be in. No pressure will be put on you but those of you in the congregation who are pastors or leaders in your church, please do not minister. Allow our ministry team to minister to you.'

I liked that. It was orderly and made sense.

The service began, very different from anything I'd experienced in the Methodist Church. We sang chorus-type things unfamiliar to me, which were projected on the slanting ceiling in front of us. What I found confusing was the way they jumped from verse to verse. I never knew whether we were singing the first verse twice, the chorus three times or had moved on to verse two. They seemed to go all over the place so I couldn't really get a good sing. How thankful I was for our orderly, traditional Methodist style of singing. However, despite the unfamiliarity of it all I felt quite at home.

For me, Ken's sermon was nothing dynamic. I'd heard better, but it was scripturally sound, humorous and very much from the heart. 'How can God work through his church if, among his people, there still remains division, hurt and pain?' he asked. I nodded, warming to this man. He was preaching what I'd preached passionately throughout my ministry. Reconciliation among God's people.

After his sermon he invited people to come forward for ministry, similar to the way I did in the services of healing and wholeness. Like me, he spoke about what people might expect, just to reassure them. 'Falling in the Spirit might not be your experience. Fine! Indeed you may not wish to receive ministry at all. That's fine, too. In fact, you might be here just as an observer. That's OK.'

Then, after a simple, down-to-earth appeal, his music team took over, playing quietly in the background, and within a few minutes I was amazed to see a couple of hundred people or more respond. Ken came forward to the microphone again, a broad grin across his face. 'Ignore what I said before about no one ministering other than our ministry team,' he said. 'If there are any ministers or pastors in the congregation tonight, could you please come forward and help us minister to these people. There are far too many for our ministry team to cope with. Ministers and pastors only, please.'

I was to learn much later that this was the first time they had made such an appeal. Two pairs of eyes either side of me turned in my direction and all my good intentions of not getting involved flew out of the window. Reluctantly I rose to my feet and made my way to the front. Every available space on the stage and up the aisles was packed with people. I found myself partially hidden down one of the side aisles. A young man, a member of the ministry team approached me.

'You're a pastor?'

'A Methodist minister.'

He smiled. 'Fine. We usually minister in pairs.' He looked around the crowded aisles. 'We might as well start where we are. Not much room to move anywhere else.'

Somewhat nervously I approached a lady of about my own age and asked her if she would like to receive ministry. She nodded. Raising my hands over her head, but not touching her, I began to pray. To my utter amazement she toppled like a felled tree and was caught by my young colleague from the ministry team. Now I understood why they ministered in pairs! I stared at the fallen figure in amazement. In all my experience, particularly in the ministry of healing, I had never, ever had such a response!

My young colleague grinned when he saw the expression on my face. 'Don't worry. She's OK. This happens every night.'

'But I didn't even touch her,' I stammered.

'I know. Most of the time we don't either. All we say is "Give them more of your Holy Spirit, Lord" and they're away. By the end of the evening the floor will be littered with bodies.'

We continued praying for the people congregated around us and sure enough, one by one they slumped to the floor. By now it seemed that the rest of the congregation were wanting to 'catch a blessing' and somehow or other my young companion and I became separated among the mass of people moving to the front or stacking chairs to make more room. I found myself standing at the rear of the church among the stacked chairs, bags, coats and belongings and for a while watched with interest all that was taking place. There were cries, sobs, shakes and even laughter as people fell under the power of the Holy Spirit. And it was the Holy Spirit, of that I had no doubt whatsoever. I was very much aware of God's presence in this place. It was the same presence I'd often experienced in our own services of healing and wholeness, and I felt very much at ease.

'But what about me?' I thought. 'I know I need to receive from God.'

Suddenly I spotted Pastor Ken only yards from where I stood. I had just plucked up the courage to move in his direction when he whizzed past me and began making more room for his flaking congregation by helping to stack the chairs around the wall. I couldn't believe it! What was he doing stacking chairs when there were people around him needing ministry? It dawned on me that I knew another minister like him. Me. Always busy doing things he shouldn't be doing. I smiled inwardly. I could identify with this man. In fact I felt I could trust him to pray for me.

After all, I'd liaised with the police when I was a social worker. They were pretty down-to-earth in their approach. He turned and as he made his way towards me I grabbed his shirtsleeve.

'Do you think you could pray for me?' I asked.

'No problem,' he assured me with a grin.

'I'm er . . . I'm a Methodist minister,' I said, almost apologetically. I don't know why I told him. It wasn't important. Perhaps it was because I believed phenomena like this didn't happen to Methodist ministers, at least not this Methodist minister, and I didn't want him to be disillusioned.

'Aye, and I'm a pastor. Makes no difference to Jesus,' he chuckled. 'He's doing what he likes around here and I think we all need to let him have his way with us no matter where we're from.'

I nodded my approval. I understood his language. Yes, this chap definitely had his head screwed on the right way!

'Let's pray.' He raised his hand above my forehead but didn't touch me and one of his team moved behind me. 'Come, Lord Jesus, come, Holy Spirit and minister to my brother. Bring more and more of your blessing.'

The thought had just crossed my mind, 'At least nothing strange will happen to me. The prayers are all I need,' when I found myself falling backward into the waiting arms of a ministry team member and being gently lowered to the floor. Then that familiar peaceful presence of Jesus seemed to wash all over me.

I returned home pleased I'd made the effort to go. I still wasn't sure what exactly had taken place when I'd fallen on the floor and had a barrage of questions to work through, but I was quite certain I would go back. Over the next few weeks I visited the Sunderland Christian Centre several times to continue my observations and became totally convinced in my own heart and mind that what was taking place was of God. I didn't understand it, but it was of God.

Not everyone felt as I did. I heard some say that the strange phenomena taking place were of the devil and therefore evil but I didn't feel that. I found Pastor Ken Gott and his wife Lois and the ministry team of Sunderland Christian Centre to be warm Christian folk, who weren't afraid to admit that this was a new experience for them and that they occasionally made mistakes while conducting the services, and hoped it hadn't caused anyone any undue stress. Their humility, warmth and desire to be open to God and his people impressed me greatly.

One Sunday morning as I preached from my prepared sermon I found myself departing from my notes and beginning to share with the congregation something of my own experience of Sunderland.

'I'll conclude by asking you a question,' I said. 'If God is wanting to touch you, are you willing to let him? Or are you going to say "no"?' A sea of mixed expressions stared back at me. 'You may not be touched in the same way the Sunderland people are but that doesn't really matter. The real question is, are you willing to receive whatever God has for you and for us here as his church?'

'That was spot on,' Joan remarked after the service, and a number of the congregation thanked me with relieved expressions on their faces.

'At least now we know you've been to Sunderland we can talk openly about it,' one of them said.

That comment decided me to call a meeting to give the folks who'd been to Sunderland a chance to discuss their experiences and hopefully try to make sense of what was going on. There were about fifteen of us at that first meeting. We listened to a tape of three Methodist ministers in Plymouth discussing with their congregations the events and phenomena of what had become known as the 'Toronto Blessing'. There were several references to the Sunderland

Christian Centre and during their question and answer time we realised they had the same queries, fears and problems we had. Our lively discussion evening ended all too soon and in all my years as a Methodist minister I'd never known such enthusiasm for another such meeting.

A fortnight later we gathered to continue where we left off. Two of my congregation in their early thirties, David and Karen, shared something of their recent visit to the Toronto church. After he'd finished talking David suggested we pray. We sat quietly praying in our comfortable chairs in the elegant living-room of another member of my congregation. It was very peaceful, so very easy to soak in like sponges the gentle presence of Jesus Christ. Then one by one we began to fall to our knees. Some openly wept, others began experiencing tingling sensations or shaking in their bodies, one or two lay prostrate on the floor in repentance and humility. It felt as if the Holy Spirit was washing over us in waves. God was doing something deep inside each one of us and there was an overwhelming desire to let him have his way.

A couple of days later I had a telephone call from a friend in one of my former churches.

'Alex? It's Colin. Have you heard about this thing in Sunderland? The Toronto Blessing, I think it's been called.'

'Yes, I have.'

'What do you think?'

I hesitated. 'Well, it's interesting and very different.'

'Would you mind coming along with me and Mary?'

'No, I'd love to, Colin. But, mind, don't expect a Methodist service and er . . . you might not like the singing. They sing these chorus, ditty things. And don't expect a detailed three-point sermon because you won't get one.'

'Oh.'

'And I'd better tell you there'll be folk jumping all over the place.'

'Jumping all over the place?'

'Aye. Well, they're Pentecostal, Assemblies of God. You know what they're like. A happy-clappy band. I'd also better mention the fact that you might end up on the floor!'

'End up on the . . .'

'Some of them grunt. The Pastor does. His wife doesn't. She jerks and shakes.'

There was silence at the other end of the telephone. 'How about Thursday night, Colin? Are you and Mary free then?'

As I put down the telephone it did occur to me that I may have gone a little overboard in my detailed description. It did sound a bit bizarre.

Convinced I was going to Sunderland simply for the sake of my friends, I wasn't expecting anything to happen to me. In fact, I'd actually told Joan and Ann I didn't really feel the need to return. I'd been there, seen it, done it and received all I needed. How wrong I was! The service was wonderful. The music and songs, not normally my cup of tea, drew me into a great time of worship and as they took up the offering it was as if they knew there were Methodists present for they sang 'O for a thousand tongues to sing', and you can't get more Methodist than that!

Colin, Mary and I sang with great gusto and I could see they were quite happy in the environment. The whole evening for me was filled with a deep time of worship and even though I had begun to realise that many Methodists had been attending these services, I couldn't have cared less who saw me. All I wanted was to worship God and receive all he had for me. So when the time came for ministry I quite comfortably moved my chair to the back of the hall, returned to the spot where I'd been sitting and waited patiently for one of the couples from the ministry team to come my way. Colin stood at the back of the hall with the chairs to observe but Mary hesitantly stood by my side, also waiting for ministry. The music group played quietly in the background and I quietly continued to worship. Then Mary gently touched my arm.

'Alex.' Her eyes were filling with tears. 'Alex, I'm . . . I'm frightened.' I took her into my arms and her whole body shook as her tears broke into deep sobs. Streams of tears ran down her face, soaking my shirt. I didn't say anything, I just held her close to me and allowed God to do whatever he was doing. But then, after a while, it was as if her tears started soaking past my shirt, right through into my body, releasing dam walls inside me. A deep sob escaped my lips and it wasn't in compassion for Mary. From the pit of my stomach tears rose till they ran in floods down my face. I cried as I have never cried before and I didn't really know why. It was only as I analysed what was going on later, that I realised it was the Lord dealing with the failures in my life, the sadnesses, the hurts, disappointments, pain and wounds. But at that moment I couldn't identify any one of them.

Since being a child in hospital, so close to death and separated from my family, I'd always tried to cope, hiding my feelings and fears even from those close to me. I'd always grasped the reins of my life with both hands, determined to be in charge, blundering through, avoiding, when I could, the hurts and pain of the world around me. But this evening there was no more avoiding. I was facing the truth. I was being released. I was finally acknowledging that God was in charge. I was allowing God to be God in my life.

Two of the ministry team began praying for Mary and more of her tears came flooding out. A moment later she lay flat on the floor at my feet. I waited. Eventually two young men came over to where I stood and as they prayed over me my hands and arms began to twitch.

'This is ridiculous!' I thought. 'Why am I twitching?' The twitch turned into a tremble then suddenly my whole body began to shake. The next thing I knew I was lying on the carpet twitching, sobbing, laughing and shaking all at the same time. But I didn't feel foolish as a good part of the congregation was behaving in a similar manner. I don't know how long I lay there, I believe it was for a good half-hour, perhaps longer. As the sobs died down and the twitching and shaking in my body subsided I was aware of a deep sense of peace stealing over me, assuring me that everything was now all right.

Eventually the strength flowed back into my body. I opened my eyes, aware of the hundreds of people lying on the floor around me. Others were sitting talking quietly in corners, regaining their strength after their powerful encounter with God, and some were collecting their belongings from the back of the hall, preparing to go home. I struggled to my feet and, as I made my way towards the back of the hall where Colin and Mary sat in deep discussion, an inner voice seemed to say, 'It is done! Now get on with the ministry I have given you!'

᎒ 23 ᎒

I stood at the front of the church trying to hide my concern. The ministry team of our healing and wholeness service seemed to be disintegrating before my very eyes and there wasn't a thing I could do about it. It was very unnerving.

One of the team members had preached brilliantly and very much from the heart. Now here she was, sitting on the row of seats at the front, visibly shaking from head to foot, her hands grasping her knees in an attempt to control this strange phenomenon that gripped her. Within minutes, another member of the team who was sitting with her was convulsed in stifled laughter. Fortunately both of them were attempting to control what was taking place and as they had their backs to the rest of the congregation, neither of them were too conspicuous.

I suddenly realised that they were experiencing the same manifestations I had seen at the Sunderland Christian Centre, and that the Holy Spirit had fallen upon them. Neither of these ladies were charismatic in their Christian outlook or experience and they had only visited the Sunderland Christian Centre once, some months ago. That this strange experience should happen to them must have been as puzzling for them as it was for me.

'Let us pray,' I heard myself saying and wondered why because I hadn't actually planned to pray in this part of the service. But considering what was taking place it would obviously be better if everyone had their eyes shut. The last thing I wanted was to scare people away. These things had to be dealt with sensitively and with explanations and understanding.

In the middle of my prayers of intercession, I suddenly had the urge to walk slowly down the aisle. I didn't consider that it was a very extraordinary thing to do as long as I didn't jerk, giggle, shake or grunt. Obedient to what I believed to be God's prompting, I moved slowly into the body of the church between the aisles, halting for a moment at the end of each row. I then invited members of the congregation to share their thoughts and prayers with me. Praying aloud in this manner was something that was unheard of, even in the healing and wholeness service, which in itself was considered quite revolutionary in the eyes of some folk. To my amazement concerns and requests flooded out into the open. Even strangers obviously felt our church a safe and comfortable place to be in and opened their hearts in prayer. I was almost moved to tears myself but that was nothing new. In the last few weeks I'd been moved to tears when conducting the wedding of folk I didn't even know! I forgot all about the shaking taking place in the front row as member after member of the congregation began quietly crying. God was at work in many different ways tonight, healing and making whole. I knew it by that perfect peace that filled our church. It was a remarkable experience.

I was sitting at my desk the following morning, catching up with the mail and the thousand and one other things that seem to accumulate on the desk of a Methodist minister, when the telephone rang.

'Hello, Alex. Cecil here. I just thought I'd give you a call to see how you were.' Before I could answer he launched into what was really on his mind.

'I see you've brought the 'Toronto Blessing' into church, then?'

'Pardon?'

'Aye. I heard all about the lass who fell over at the previous healing service when you prayed for her. Then the prayers you did last night, walking down the aisle and getting everybody involved. Sneaky, but nice.'

I struggled to control the laughter welling up inside me. 'I would hardly have called the open time of prayer when I walked down the aisle, the 'Toronto Blessing,' Cecil.' But even as I spoke it occurred to me that for some people that type of open prayer and the movement of the Holy Spirit in the church was a new experience. 'You enjoyed the service though, Cecil?'

'Different,' he said reservedly. 'Good turn out. Shame one or two of your team took ill, though. Shakin' like the dickens, they were. Flu no doubt. Lot of it about.'

I was relieved when we'd finished the business in hand and I was able to put the telephone down and explode with laughter.

The episode in the healing service where one of the ladies in the congregation had fallen over when we'd prayed with her had come as no surprise to me. Although nothing like that had ever happened before, I had gone to the service that evening expecting something different to take place. I'd walked into the church, handing the reins of the service and all who were to take part into God's hands, and that night, I had to confess, he'd done quite well!

I'm not anxious to propagate either the 'Toronto Blessing' or the 'Sunderland experience'. All I know is that God is speaking, refreshing, cleansing and empowering his people and that a group of us who, like myself, have had the experience of what is commonly referred to as the 'Toronto Blessing', are meeting together regularly to explore further what he has to say. Most of them describe what has happened to them as 'being turned inside out'. I don't really understand it but it seems a pretty fair description of what's happening to me. It's a bit like the time the call to the healing ministry came. I was for a long time uncertain, ignorant and cautious. Then very gradually and prayerfully we moved forward to discover what God was saying to us and we're doing the same thing now.

When God decided to call me into the ministry of healing I couldn't believe he'd got the right person. I'm noisy, boisterous, outspoken and always rushing in where angels fear to tread, but I suppose he knew what he was doing, so now I try to put my trust in him even if I do ask a lot of questions and get it wrong sometimes. 'You know, God, if only you would tell me a bit more, speak a bit louder, it would be so much easier to carry out the things you want me to do. Do you always have to be so secretive? I want to know what's happening tomorrow, never mind next week, but then I've always been impatient and eager to get on with life, so perhaps it's best I don't know too much beforehand.'

Talking to God is a lot easier these days as well. It's a bit like talking to my wife, except there's no backchat!

I was preparing a sermon the other week from John 15:4. 'I am the vine and you are the branches.' It's a favourite passage of mine. It reminds me that without him I am nothing. As I meditated on the text it seemed as though the words of Jesus sprang out from the pages and hit me. 'I chose you, you did not choose me.' That's right! He chose me! Yet I sometimes act as though I'm the one in charge, as if, since I'd given my life to him, I'd chosen him.

As I reflected back on my life it dawned on me that the greatest times of impact have been when I've let God be God in my life. But time and time again, I'm ashamed to say, I've battled against his will because I like to be in control.

However, I do pray, Father, that whatever the future may have in store for me, that your will, your perfect will, will always be done – eventually!